ITALIAN COOKBOOK 2022

QUICK, TASTY AND AUTHENTIC REGIONAL RECIPES

GIULIA DESIO

PAPPAI PURU!

TABLE OF CONTENTS

Savory Pie Pastry 9

Spinach Ricotta Tart 12

Leek Tart 14

Mozzarella, Basil, and Roasted Pepper Sandwiches 16

Spinach and Robiola Sandwiches 18

Riviera Sandwich 20

Tuna and Roasted Pepper Triangle Sandwiches 23

Prosciutto and Fig Triangle Sandwiches 25

Amaretto Baked Apples 26

Livia's Apple Cake 28

Apricots in Lemon Syrup 31

Berries with Lemon and Sugar 33

Strawberries with Balsamic Vinegar 35

Raspberries with Mascarpone and Balsamic Vinegar 37

Cherries in Barolo 39

Hot Roasted Chestnuts 41

Fig Preserves 43

Chocolate-Dipped Figs 45

Figs in Wine Syrup 47

Dora's Baked Figs 49

Honeydew in Mint Syrup 51

Oranges in Orange Syrup 52

Oranges Gratinéed with Zabaglione 54

White Peaches in Asti Spumante 56

Peaches in Red Wine 57

Amaretti-Stuffed Peaches 58

Pears in Orange Sauce 60

Pears with Marsala and Cream 62

Pears with Warm Chocolate Sauce 64

Rum-Spiced Pears 66

Spiced Pears with Pecorino 68

Poached Pears with Gorgonzola 70

Pear or Apple Pudding Cake 72

Warm Fruit Compote 75

Venetian Caramelized Fruit 77

Fruit with Honey and Grappa 79

Winter Fruit Salad 81

Grilled Summer Fruit 83

Warm Ricotta with Honey 85

Coffee Ricotta 86

Mascarpone and Peaches 88

Chocolate Foam with Raspberries 90

Tiramisù 92

Strawberry Tiramisù 95

Italian Trifle 97

Zabaglione 99

Chocolate Zabaglione 101

Chilled Zabaglione with Berries 103

Lemon Gelatin 105

Orange Rum Gelatin 108

Espresso Gelatin 110

Panna Cotta 112

Butter Rings 115

Lemon Knots 117

Spice Cookies 120

Wafer Cookies 122

Sweet Ravioli 125

"Ugly-but-Good" Cookies 128

Jam Spots 130

Double-Chocolate Nut Biscotti 132

Chocolate Kisses 135

No-Bake Chocolate "Salame" 138

Prato Biscuits 140

Umbrian Fruit and Nut Biscotti 142

Lemon Nut Biscotti 145

Walnut Biscotti 147

Almond Macaroons 149

Pine Nut Macaroons 152

Hazelnut Bars 154

Walnut Butter Cookies 156

Rainbow Cookies 158

Christmas Fig Cookies 162

Almond Brittle 166

Sicilian Nut Rolls 168

Sponge Cake 171

Citrus Sponge Cake 173

Lemon Olive-Oil Cake 176

Marble Cake 178

Rum Cake 181

Grandmother's Cake 184

Apricot Almond Cake 188

Summer Fruit Torte 191

Autumn Fruit Torte 193

Polenta and Pear Cake 195

Ricotta Cheesecake 198

Sicilian Ricotta Cake 200

Ricotta Crumb Cake 203

Easter Wheat-Berry Cake 206

Chocolate Hazelnut Cake 211

Chocolate Almond Cake 215

Chocolate Orange Torte 218

Savory Pie Pastry

Pasta Frolla Salata

Makes one 9- to 10-inch pie shell

A savory pie similar to a quiche can be made with cheese, eggs, and vegetables. These pies are good at room temperature or hot, and can be served as a piatto unico—one-dish meal—or as an appetizer. This pastry is good for all types of savory pies.

I roll out this dough between two sheets of plastic wrap. It prevents the dough from sticking to the board and rolling pin, so it is not necessary to add more flour, which can toughen the dough. To ensure that the crust is crisp on the bottom, I partially prebake the shell before adding the filling.

1½ cups all-purpose flour

1 teaspoon salt

½ cup (1 stick) unsalted butter, at room temperature

1 egg yolk

3 to 4 tablespoons ice water

1. Prepare the dough: Combine the flour and salt in a large bowl. With a pastry blender or a fork, cut in the butter until the mixture resembles coarse crumbs.

2. Beat the egg yolk together with 2 tablespoons of the water. Sprinkle the mixture over the flour. Mix together lightly until the dough is evenly moistened and comes together without being sticky. Add the remaining water if needed.

3. Shape the dough into a disk. Wrap in plastic wrap. Refrigerate 30 minutes or overnight.

4. If the dough has been refrigerated overnight, let it stand at room temperature 20 to 30 minutes before rolling it out. Place the dough between two sheets of plastic wrap and roll it out to a 12-inch circle, turning the dough and rearranging the plastic wrap with each turn. Remove the top sheet of plastic wrap. Using the remaining sheet to lift the dough, center the dough with the plastic up in a 9- to 10-inch tart pan with a removable base. Peel off the plastic wrap. Gently press the dough into the base and along the sides.

5. Roll the rolling pin over the top of the pan and trim off the overhanging dough. Press the dough against the side of the pan

to create a rim higher than the edge of the pan. Chill the pastry shell in the refrigerator 30 minutes.

6. Place the oven rack in the lower third of the oven. Preheat the oven to 450°F. With a fork, prick the bottom of the tart shell at 1-inch intervals. Bake for 5 minutes, then prick the dough again. Bake until just set, 10 minutes more. Remove the shell from the oven. Cool on a rack 10 minutes.

Spinach Ricotta Tart

Crostata di Spinaci

Makes 8 servings

I had a tart like this at Ferrara, a favorite restaurant in Rome. Something like a quiche, it is made with ricotta for extra creaminess. It is great for a lunch or brunch dish, served with a salad and chilled pinot grigio wine.

    1 recipe Savory Pie Pastry

Filling

1 pound spinach, trimmed and rinsed

¼ cup water

1½ cups whole or part-skim ricotta

½ cup heavy cream

¾ cup freshly grated Parmigiano-Reggiano

2 large eggs, beaten

¼ teaspoon freshly grated nutmeg

Salt and freshly ground black pepper

1. Prepare and partially bake the crust. Reduce the oven temperature to 375°F.

2. Meanwhile, prepare the filling. Put the spinach in a large pot over medium heat with the water. Cover and cook 2 to 3 minutes or until wilted and tender. Drain and cool. Wrap the spinach in a lint-free cloth and squeeze out as much water as possible. Finely chop the spinach.

3. In a large bowl, beat together the spinach, ricotta, cream, cheese, eggs, nutmeg, and salt and pepper to taste. Scrape the mixture into the prepared tart shell.

4. Bake 35 to 40 minutes or until the filling is set and lightly browned.

5. Cool the tart in the pan 10 minutes. Remove the outer rim and place the tart on a serving dish. Serve warm or at room temperature.

Leek Tart

Crostata di Porri

Makes 6 to 8 servings

I had this tart at an enoteca, or wine bar, in Bologna. The nutty flavor of the Parmigiano and the cream enhance the sweet flavor of the leeks. It can also be made with sautéed mushrooms or peppers instead of the leeks.

    1 recipe Savory Pie Pastry

Filling

4 medium leeks, about 1¼ pounds

3 tablespoons unsalted butter

Salt

2 large eggs

¾ cup heavy cream

⅓ cup freshly grated Parmigiano-Reggiano

Freshly grated nutmeg

Freshly ground black pepper

1. Prepare and partially bake the crust. Reduce the oven temperature to 375°F.

2. Prepare the filling: Trim off the roots and most of the green tops of the leeks. Cut them in half lengthwise and rinse them very well between each layer under cold running water. Cut the leeks into thin crosswise slices.

3. In a large skillet, melt the butter over medium heat. Add the leeks and a pinch of salt. Cook, stirring often, until the leeks are tender when pierced with a knife, about 20 minutes. Remove the pan from the heat and let cool.

4. In a medium bowl, beat together the eggs, cream, cheese, and a pinch of nutmeg. Stir in the leeks and pepper to taste.

5. Scrape the mixture into the partially baked tart shell. Bake 35 to 40 minutes or until the filling is set. Serve warm or at room temperature.

Mozzarella, Basil, and Roasted Pepper Sandwiches

Panini di Mozzarella

Makes 2 servings

I sometimes make this sandwich substituting arugula for the basil and prosciutto for the red peppers.

4 ounces fresh mozzarella cheese, cut into 8 slices

4 slices country bread

4 fresh basil leaves

¼ cup roasted red or yellow bell peppers, cut into thin strips

1. Trim the mozzarella slices to fit the bread. If the mozzarella is juicy, pat it dry. Lay half the cheese in a single layer on two slices of bread.

2. Arrange the basil leaves and peppers on the cheese and top with the remaining mozzarella. Place the remaining bread on top and press down firmly with your hands.

3. Preheat a sandwich press or stove-top grill pan. Place the sandwiches in the press and cook until toasted, about 4 to 5

minutes. If using a grill pan, place a heavy weight such as a frying pan on top. Turn the sandwiches when browned on one side, cover with the weight, and toast on the second side. Serve hot.

Spinach and Robiola Sandwiches

Panino di Spinaci e Robiola

Makes 2 servings

Focaccia adds nice flavor and texture to pressed panini. Other greens can be substituted for the spinach, or use leftover vegetables. For the cheese, I like to use robiola, a soft creamy cheese made from cow's, goat's, or sheep's milk, or a combination, from Piedmont and Lombardy. Other possibilities are fresh goat cheese or even whipped cream cheese. Add a drop or two of truffle oil to the filling for an earthy flavor and a touch of luxury.

1 (10-ounce) package fresh spinach

4 ounces fresh robiola, or substitute goat cheese

Truffle oil (optional)

2 serving-size squares or wedges of fresh focaccia

1. Put the spinach in a large pot over medium heat with $1/4$ cup of water. Cover and cook 2 to 3 minutes or until wilted and tender. Drain and cool. Wrap the spinach in a lint-free cloth and squeeze out as much water as possible.

2. Finely chop the spinach and place it in a medium bowl. Add the cheese and mash the spinach into the cheese. Add a drop or two of truffle oil, if you like.

3. With a long serrated knife, carefully cut the focaccia in half horizontally. Spread the mixture on the inside of the bottom halves of the focaccia. Place the tops on the sandwiches and flatten gently.

4. Preheat a sandwich press or stove-top grill pan. If using a press, place the sandwiches in the press and cook until toasted, about 4 to 5 minutes. If using a grill pan, place the sandwiches on the pan, then a heavy weight, such as a frying pan, on top.

5. When browned on one side, turn the sandwiches, cover with the weight, and toast on the second side. Serve hot.

Riviera Sandwich

Panino della Riviera

Makes 4 servings

The geographic border dividing Italy and France does not also signify a distinction in the food eaten on either side. With their similar climate and geography, people living along the Italian and French coasts share very similar food customs. A case in point is the French pan bagnat and Italian pane bagnato, meaning "bathed bread," which is sometimes called a Riviera sandwich in Italy. This hearty sandwich, bathed in a lively vinaigrette dressing, is stuffed with tuna and roasted peppers in France. On the Italian side of the border, mozzarella stands in for the tuna, and anchovies are added, but the rest is pretty much the same. This is the perfect sandwich to take on a picnic, because the flavors marry well, and it only gets better as it stands.

1 loaf Italian bread, about 12 inches long

Dressing

1 garlic clove, very finely chopped

¼ cup olive oil

2 tablespoons vinegar

½ teaspoon dried oregano, crumbled

Salt and freshly ground black pepper

2 ripe tomatoes, sliced

1 (2-ounce) can anchovies

8 ounces sliced mozzarella

2 peeled and seeded roasted peppers with their juice

12 oil-cured olives, pitted and chopped

1. Cut the bread loaf in half lengthwise and remove the soft bread inside.

2. In a small bowl, whisk together the dressing ingredients and pour half the dressing over the cut sides of the bread. Layer the bottom half of the bread with the tomatoes, anchovies, mozzarella, roasted peppers, and olives, drizzling each layer with some of the dressing.

3. Place the top on the sandwich and press it together. Wrap in foil and cover with a board or heavy pan. Let stand at room temperature up to 2 hours or store in the refrigerator overnight.

4. Slice into 3-inch-wide sandwiches. Serve at room temperature.

Tuna and Roasted Pepper Triangle Sandwiches

Tramezzini al Tonno e Peperoni

Makes 3 sandwiches

Some of the same flavors of the hearty Riviera sandwich find their way into this delicate triangle sandwich I tasted at a favorite Roman café. The tuna was seasoned with fennel seeds, but I like to substitute fennel pollen, which is nothing more than ground-up fennel seeds, but has more flavor. A lot of chefs are using it these days, and it can be found in gourmet shops specializing in dried herbs as well as on Internet sites. If you can't find fennel pollen, substitute fennel seeds, which you can grind yourself in a spice grinder or chop with a knife.

1 small roasted red pepper, drained and cut into thin strips

Extra-virgin olive oil

Salt

1 (3½-ounce) can Italian tuna packed in olive oil

2 tablespoons mayonnaise

1 to 2 teaspoons fresh lemon juice

1 tablespoon chopped green onion

1 teaspoon fennel pollen

4 slices good-quality white sandwich bread

1. Toss the roasted pepper with a little oil and salt.

2. Drain the tuna and place it in a bowl. Mash the tuna well with a fork. Blend in the mayonnaise, lemon juice to taste, and green onion.

3. Spread the tuna on two of the bread slices. Top with the pepper strips. Cover with the remaining bread, pressing down slightly.

4. With a large chef's knife, trim off the bread crusts. Cut the sandwiches in half diagonally to form two triangles. Serve immediately or cover tightly with plastic wrap and refrigerate until ready to serve.

Prosciutto and Fig Triangle Sandwiches

Tramezzini di Prosciutto e Fichi

Makes 2 sandwiches

The saltiness of the prosciutto and sweetness of the fig jam offer a pleasant contrast in this sandwich. It is very good as an appetizer if you cut it into quarters. Serve it with sparkling Prosecco.

Unsalted butter, at room temperature

4 slices good-quality white sandwich bread

About 2 tablespoons fig jam

4 thin slices imported Italian prosciutto

1. Spread a little butter on one side of each slice of bread. Spread about 2 teaspoons fig jam over the butter on each slice.

2. Arrange two slices of prosciutto on half of the slices. Place the remaining slices of bread jam-side-down on the prosciutto.

3. With a large chef's knife, trim off the bread crusts. Cut the sandwiches in half diagonally to form two triangles. Serve immediately or cover with plastic wrap and refrigerate.

Amaretto Baked Apples

Mele al'Amaretto

Makes 6 servings

Amaretto is a sweet liqueur; amaretti are crisp cookies. Both of these Italian products are flavored with two kinds of almonds—the familiar variety, plus a slightly bitter almond that is not eaten on its own, though it is frequently used in Italy to flavor desserts. Amaro means "bitter," and both the liqueur and the cookies take their name from these almonds. Both are widely available—the cookies in specialty shops and by mail order and the liqueur in many liquor stores.

The most familiar brand of amaretti cookies is packaged in distinctive red tins or boxes. The cookies are wrapped in pairs in pastel tissue paper. There are other brands of amaretti that pack the cookies loose in bags. I always have amaretti in the house. They keep a long time and are nice with a cup of tea, or as an ingredient in a number of sweet and savory dishes.

Golden delicious are the apples I prefer for baking. The locally grown ones are sweet and crisp, yet they hold their shape nicely when baked.

6 baking apples, such as golden delicious

6 amaretti cookies

6 tablespoons sugar

2 tablespoons unsalted butter

6 tablespoons amaretto or rum

1. Place a rack in the center of the oven. Preheat the oven to 375°F. Butter a baking dish just large enough to hold the apples standing upright.

2. Remove the apple cores and peel the apples about two-thirds of the way down from the stem end.

3. Place the amaretti cookies in a plastic bag and crush them gently with a heavy object, such as a rolling pin. In a medium bowl, blend the crumbs with the sugar and butter.

4. Stuff a little of the mixture into the center of each apple. Spoon the amaretto over the apples. Pour 1 cup water around the apples.

5. Bake 45 minutes or until the apples are tender when pierced with a knife. Serve warm or at room temperature.

Livia's Apple Cake

Torta di Mele alla Livia

Makes 8 servings

My friend Livia Colantonio lives in Umbria on a farm called Podernovo. The farm raises Chianina cattle, grows a variety of wine grapes, and bottles wine under the Castello delle Regine label.

Guests can stay in one of the beautifully restored guesthouses at Podernovo, which is just 45 minutes from Rome, and enjoy a restful vacation. Livia makes this simple but sensational "cake" that is always good after a fall or winter meal. It isn't a cake in the traditional sense, because it is made almost entirely of apples, with just a few cookie crumbs between the layers to hold some of the fruit juices. Serve it with a dollop of whipped cream or rum-raisin ice cream.

You will need a round pan or baking dish 9 inches wide by 3 inches deep. Use a cake pan, or a casserole or soufflé dish, but do not use a springform pan because the apple juices will leak out.

12 amaretti cookies

3 pounds golden delicious, Granny Smith, or other firm apples (about 6 large)

½ cup sugar

1. Place the amaretti cookies in a plastic bag and crush them gently with a heavy object, such as a rolling pin. You should have about ¾ cup of crumbs.

2. Peel the apples and cut them into quarters lengthwise. Cut the quarters into ⅛-inch-thick slices.

3. Place a rack in the center of the oven. Preheat the oven to 350°F. Generously butter a 9 × 3–inch round baking pan or a tube pan. Line the bottom of the pan with a circle of parchment paper. Butter the paper.

4. Make a layer of apples overlapping slightly in the bottom of the pan. Sprinkle with a little of the crumbs and sugar. Alternate layers of the remaining apple slices in the pan with the remaining crumbs and sugar. The apple slices do not have to be arranged neatly. Place a sheet of foil over the top, molding it over the rim of the pan.

5. Bake the apples 1½ hours. Uncover and bake 30 minutes more or until the apples are tender when pierced with a knife and

diminished in volume. Transfer the pan to a wire rack. Let cool at least 15 minutes. Run a knife around the edge of the pan. Holding the pan with a pot holder in one hand, place a flat serving plate over the top of the pan. Invert them both, so the apples transfer onto the plate.

6. Serve at room temperature, cut into wedges. Cover with an inverted bowl and store in the refrigerator up to 3 days.

Apricots in Lemon Syrup

Albicocche al Limone

Makes 6 servings

Perfectly ripe apricots really need no enhancement, but if you have some that are less than perfect, try cooking them in a simple lemon syrup. Serve the poached apricots chilled, possibly with amaretto-flavored whipped cream.

1 cup cold water

¼ cup sugar, or to taste

2 (2-inch) strips lemon zest

2 tablespoons fresh lemon juice

1 pound apricots (about 8)

1. In a saucepan or skillet large enough to hold the apricot halves in a single layer, combine the water, sugar, zest, and juice. Bring to a simmer over medium-low heat and cook, swirling the pan once or twice, for 10 minutes.

2. Following the line on the apricots, cut them in half and remove the pits. Place the halves in the simmering syrup. Cook, turning once, until the fruit is tender, about 5 minutes.

3. Let the apricots cool briefly in the syrup, then cover and store in the refrigerator. Serve chilled.

Berries with Lemon and Sugar

Frutti di Bosco al Limone

Makes 4 servings

Fresh lemon juice and sugar bring out all the flavor of berries. Try this with just one berry variety or a combination. Top the dressed berries with a scoop of lemon ice or sorbet if you like.

One of my favorite berries, the tiny wild strawberry (fragoline del bosco), is common in Italy but not widely available here. Wild strawberries have a mouthwatering strawberry aroma and are easy to grow in a flowerpot. Seeds are available from many catalog companies, and you can buy the plants at many nurseries here in the United States.

1 cup sliced strawberries

1 cup blackberries

1 cup blueberries

1 cup raspberries

Freshly squeezed lemon juice (about 2 tablespoons)

Sugar (about 1 tablespoon)

1. In a large bowl, gently toss the berries together. Drizzle with the lemon juice and sugar to taste. Taste and adjust seasoning.

2. Place the berries in shallow serving dishes. Serve immediately.

Strawberries with Balsamic Vinegar

Fragole al Balsamico

Makes 2 servings

If you can find the little wild strawberries known in Italian as fragoline del bosco, use them in this dessert. But ordinary fresh strawberries, too, will benefit from a quick marinate in aged balsamic vinegar. Like a sprinkle of fresh lemon juice on a piece of fish, or salt on a steak, the intense sweet-and-tangy flavor of balsamic vinegar enhances many foods. Think of it as a condiment rather than as a vinegar.

You probably will have to buy aged balsamic vinegar at a specialty store. In the New York area, one of my favorite sources is Di Palo Fine Foods on Grand Street in Little Italy (see Sources). Louis Di Palo is a walking encyclopedia on balsamic vinegar, as well as just about any other food product imported from Italy. The first time I asked for balsamico, he brought out several bottles and offered everyone in the shop samples as he explained each one.

The best balsamico is made in the provinces of Modena and Reggio in Emilia-Romagna. Smooth, complex, and syrupy, it tastes more like a rich liqueur than a harsh vinegar, and it is often drunk as a cordial.

Look for the words Aceto Balsamico Tradizionale on the label. Though it is expensive, a little bit goes a long way.

1 pint wild or cultivated strawberries, sliced if large

2 tablespoons best-quality aged balsamic vinegar, or to taste

2 tablespoons sugar

In a medium bowl, toss the strawberries with the vinegar and sugar. Let stand 15 minutes before serving.

Raspberries with Mascarpone and Balsamic Vinegar

Lampone con Mascarpone e Balsamico

Makes 4 servings

Always rinse delicate raspberries just before you are ready to use them—if you rinse them earlier, the moisture could cause them to spoil more quickly. Before serving them, look them over and discard those that show any signs of mold. Store berries in an uncovered shallow container in the refrigerator, but use them as soon as possible after purchasing them, as they deteriorate rapidly.

Mascarpone is a thick, smooth cream that is called a cheese, though it has only the slightest cheesy tang. It has a texture similar to sour cream, or slightly thicker. If you prefer, crème fraîche, ricotta, or sour cream can be substituted.

1½ cups mascarpone

About ¼ cup sugar

1 to 2 tablespoons best-quality aged balsamic vinegar

2 cups raspberries, lightly rinsed and dried

1. In a small bowl, whisk the mascarpone and sugar until well blended. Stir in the balsamic vinegar to taste. Let stand 15 minutes and stir again.

2. Divide the raspberries among 4 goblets or serving bowls. Top with the mascarpone and serve immediately.

Cherries in Barolo

Ciliege al Barolo

Makes 4 servings

Here, sweet, ripe cherries are simmered Piedmont style in Barolo or another full-bodied red wine.

¾ cup sugar

1 cup Barolo or other dry red wine

1 pound ripe sweet cherries, pitted

1 cup heavy or whipping cream, well chilled

1. At least 20 minutes before you are ready to whip the cream, place a large bowl and the beaters of an electric mixer in the refrigerator.

2. In a large saucepan, combine the sugar and wine. Bring to a simmer and cook 5 minutes.

3. Add the cherries. After the liquid returns to a simmer, cook until the cherries are tender when pierced with a knife, about 10 minutes more. Let cool.

4. Just before serving, remove the bowl and beaters from the refrigerator. Pour the cream into the bowl and whip the cream at high speed until it holds its shape softly when the beaters are lifted, about 4 minutes.

5. Spoon the cherries into serving bowls. Serve at room temperature or slightly chilled with whipped cream.

Hot Roasted Chestnuts

Caldarroste

Makes 8 servings

St. Martin's Day, November 11, is celebrated all over Italy with hot roasted chestnuts and newly made red wine. The celebration marks not only the feast day of a beloved saint who was known for his kindness to the poor, but also the end of the growing season, the day the earth goes into repose for winter.

Roasted chestnuts are also a classic finishing touch to winter holiday meals throughout Italy. I put them in the oven to cook when we sit down to dinner, and by the time we are finished with our main course, they are ready to eat.

1 pound fresh chestnuts

1. Place a rack in the center of the oven. Preheat the oven to 425°F. Rinse the chestnuts and pat them dry. Place the chestnuts flat-side down on a cutting board. Carefully cut an X on the top of each with the tip of a small sharp knife.

2. Place the chestnuts on a large sheet of heavy-duty aluminum foil. Fold one end over the other to enclose the chestnuts. Fold

the ends over to seal. Place the package in a baking pan. Roast the chestnuts until tender when pierced with a small knife, about 45 to 60 minutes.

3. Transfer the foil package to a cooling rack. Leave the chestnuts wrapped in the foil for 10 minutes. Serve hot.

Fig Preserves

Marmellata di Fichi

Makes 1½ pints

Fig trees, both domesticated and wild, grow all over Italy, except in the northernmost regions where it is too cold. Because they are so sweet and widely available, figs are used in many desserts, especially in southern Italy. Ripe figs do not keep well, so when they are abundant in late summer they are preserved in several different ways. In Puglia, the figs are cooked with water to make thick, sweet syrup that is used for desserts. Figs are also dried in the sun or turned into fig preserves.

A small batch of fig preserves is easy to make and can be stored for a month in the refrigerator. For longer storage, the jam should be canned (following safe canning methods) or frozen. Serve it as a complement to a cheese course or for breakfast on buttered walnut bread.

1½ pounds fresh ripe figs, rinsed and dried

2 cups sugar

2 strips lemon zest

1. Peel the figs and cut them into quarters. Place them in a medium bowl with sugar and lemon zest. Stir well. Cover and refrigerate overnight.

2. The next day, transfer the contents of the bowl to a large heavy saucepan. Bring to a simmer over medium heat. Cook, stirring occasionally, until the mixture thickens slightly, about 5 minutes. To test if the mixture is thick enough, place a drop of the slightly cooled liquid between your thumb and index finger. If the mixture forms a thread when the thumb and finger are slightly separated, the preserves are ready.

3. Spoon into sterilized jars and store in the refrigerator up to 30 days.

Chocolate-Dipped Figs

Fichi al Cioccolato

Makes 8 to 10 servings

Moist dried figs stuffed with nuts and dipped in chocolate are nice as a little after-dinner treat.

I like to buy candied orange peel at Kalustyan's, a shop in New York City that specializes in spices, dried fruits, and nuts. Because they sell a lot of it, it is always fresh and full of flavor. Many other specialty shops sell good candied orange peel. You can also order it by mail (see Sources). Supermarket candied orange peel and other fruits are chopped into small bits and usually dry and tasteless.

18 moist dried figs (about 1 pound)

18 toasted almonds

½ cup candied orange peel

4 ounces bittersweet chocolate, chopped or broken into small pieces

2 tablespoons unsalted butter

1. Line a tray with wax paper and set a wire cooling rack on top. Make a small slit in the base of each fig. Insert an almond and a piece of orange peel into the figs. Pinch the slit closed.

2. In the top half of a double boiler set over simmering water, melt the chocolate and butter, about 5 minutes. Remove from the heat and stir until smooth. Let stand 5 minutes.

3. Dip each fig in the melted chocolate and place on the wire rack. When all of the figs have been dipped, place the tray in the refrigerator to set the chocolate, about 1 hour.

4. Place the figs in an airtight container, separating each layer with wax paper. Store in the refrigerator up to 30 days.

Figs in Wine Syrup

Fichi alla Contadina

Makes 8 servings

Dried calimyrna and mission figs from California are moist and plump. Either variety can be used for this recipe. After poaching, they are good as is, or served with ice cream or whipped cream. They also go well with gorgonzola cheese.

1 cup vin santo, Marsala, or dry red wine

2 tablespoons honey

2 (2-inch) strips lemon zest

18 moist dried figs (about 1 pound)

1. In a medium saucepan, combine the vin santo, honey, and lemon zest. Bring to a simmer over low heat and cook 1 minute.

2. Add the figs and cold water to cover. Bring the liquid to a simmer over low heat and cover the pot. Cook until the figs are tender, about 10 minutes.

3. With a slotted spoon, transfer the figs from the pot to a bowl. Cook the liquid, uncovered, until reduced and slightly thickened, about 5 minutes. Pour the syrup over the figs and let cool. Refrigerate at least 1 hour and up to 3 days. Serve slightly chilled.

Dora's Baked Figs

Fichi al Forno

Makes 2 dozen

Dried figs stuffed with nuts are a Pugliese specialty. This recipe is from my friend Dora Marzovilla, who serves them as an after-dinner treat at her family's New York restaurant, I Trulli. Serve the figs with a glass of dessert wine, such as Moscato di Pantelleria.

24 moist dried figs (about 1½ pounds), stem ends removed

24 toasted almonds

1 tablespoon fennel seeds

¼ cup bay leaves

1. Place a rack in the center of the oven. Preheat the oven to 350°F. Remove the hard stem ends from each fig. With a small knife, cut a slit in the base of the figs. Insert an almond in the figs and pinch the slit closed.

2. Arrange the figs on a baking sheet and bake 15 to 20 minutes or until lightly browned. Let cool on a wire rack.

3. Make a layer of the figs in a 1-quart airtight plastic or glass container. Sprinkle with some of the fennel seeds. Top with a layer of bay leaves. Repeat the layering until all of the ingredients are used. Cover and store in a cool place (but not the refrigerator) at least 1 week before serving.

Honeydew in Mint Syrup

Melone alla Menta

Makes 4 servings

After a big fish dinner at a seaside restaurant in Sicily, we were served this cool combination of honeydew melon bathed in a fresh mint syrup.

1 cup cold water

½ cup sugar

½ cup packed fresh spearmint leaves, plus more for garnish

8 to 12 slices peeled ripe honeydew melon

1. In a saucepan, combine the water, sugar, and mint leaves. Bring to a simmer and cook 1 minute or until the leaves are wilted. Remove from the heat. Let cool, then pass the syrup through a fine-mesh strainer into a bowl to strain out the mint leaves.

2. Place the melon on a serving platter and pour the syrup over the melon. Chill in the refrigerator briefly. Serve garnished with mint leaves.

Oranges in Orange Syrup

Arancia Marinate

Makes 8 servings

Juicy oranges in a sweet syrup are a perfect dessert after a rich meal. I especially like to serve these in winter when fresh oranges are at their best. Arranged on a platter, the oranges look very pretty with their topping of orange zest strips and glistening syrup. As a variation, cut the oranges into wedges and combine them with sliced ripe pineapple. Serve the orange sauce over all.

8 large navel oranges

1¼ cups sugar

2 tablespoons orange brandy or liqueur

1. Scrub the oranges with a brush. Trim off the ends. With a vegetable peeler, peel off the colored part of the orange skin (the zest) in wide strips. Avoid digging into the bitter white pith. Stack the zest strips and cut them into narrow matchstick pieces.

2. Remove the white pith from the oranges. Place the oranges on a serving platter.

3. Bring a small saucepan of water to a boil. Add the orange zest and bring to a simmer. Cook 1 minute. Drain the zest and rinse under cool water. Repeat. (This will help to remove some of the bitterness from the zest.)

4. Place the sugar and 1/4 cup of water in another small saucepan over medium heat. Bring the mixture to a boil. Cook until the sugar is melted and the syrup thickens, about 3 minutes. Stir in the orange zest and cook 3 minutes more. Let cool.

5. Add the orange brandy to the contents of the pot. With a fork, remove the orange zest from the syrup and pile it on top of the oranges. Spoon on the syrup. Cover and chill up to 3 hours until ready to serve.

Oranges Gratinéed with Zabaglione

Arancia allo Zabaglione

Makes 4 servings

Gratiné is a French word meaning to brown the surface of a dish. Usually it applies to savory foods that are sprinkled with bread crumbs or cheese to help them brown.

Zabaglione is typically served plain or as a sauce for fruit or cake. Here it is spooned over oranges and broiled briefly until it browns slightly and forms a creamy topping. Bananas, kiwis, berries, or other soft fruits can also be prepared this way.

6 navel oranges, peeled and thinly sliced

Zabaglione

1 large egg

2 large egg yolks

⅓ cup sugar

⅓ cup dry or sweet Marsala

1. Preheat the broiler. Arrange the orange slices in a flameproof baking dish, overlapping slightly.

2. Prepare the zabaglione: Fill a small saucepan or the bottom of a double boiler with 2 inches of water. Bring it to a simmer over low heat. In a bowl larger than the rim of the pan or the top of the double boiler, combine the egg, yolks, sugar, and Marsala. Beat with a hand-held electric beater until foamy. Place over the pan of simmering water. Beat until the mixture is pale-colored and holds a soft shape when the beaters are lifted, about 5 minutes.

3. Spread the zabaglione over the oranges. Put the dish under the broiler 1 to 2 minutes or until the zabaglione is browned in spots. Serve immediately.

White Peaches in Asti Spumante

Pesche Bianche in Asti Spumante

Makes 4 servings

Asti Spumante is a sweet, sparkling dessert wine from Piedmont in northwestern Italy. It has a delicate orange-blossom flavor and aroma that comes from muscat grapes. If you can't find white peaches, yellow peaches will work well or substitute another summer fruit, such as nectarines, plums, or apricots.

4 large ripe white peaches

1 tablespoon sugar

8 ounces chilled Asti Spumante

1. Peel and pit the peaches. Cut them into thin slices.

2. Toss the peaches with the sugar and let stand 10 minutes.

3. Spoon the peaches into goblets or parfait glasses. Pour on the Asti Spumante and serve immediately.

Peaches in Red Wine

Pesche al Vino Rosso

Makes 4 servings

I remember watching my grandfather cutting up his homegrown white peaches to soak in a pitcher of red wine. The sweet peach juices tamed any roughness in the wine. White peaches are my favorite, but yellow peaches or nectarines are good too.

⅓ cup sugar, or to taste

2 cups fruity red wine

4 ripe peaches

1. In a medium bowl, combine the sugar and wine.

2. Cut the peaches in half and remove the pits. Cut the peaches into bite-size pieces. Stir them into the wine. Cover and refrigerate 2 to 3 hours.

3. Spoon the peaches and wine into goblets and serve.

Amaretti-Stuffed Peaches

Pesche al Forno

Makes 4 servings

This is a favorite dessert from Piedmont. Serve it drizzled with heavy cream or topped with a scoop of ice cream.

8 medium peaches, not too ripe

8 amaretti cookies

2 tablespoons softened unsalted butter

2 tablespoons sugar

1 large egg

1. Place a rack in the center of the oven. Preheat the oven to 375°F. Butter a baking dish large enough to hold the peach halves in a single layer.

2. Place the amaretti cookies in a plastic bag and crush them gently with a heavy object, such as a rolling pin. You should have about $1/2$ cup. In a medium bowl, mix together the butter and sugar and stir in the crumbs.

3. Following the line around the peaches, cut them in half and remove the pits. With a grapefruit spoon or a melon baller, scoop out a little of the peach flesh from the center to widen the opening and add it to the crumb mixture. Stir the egg into the mixture.

4. Arrange the peach halves cut sides up in the dish. Spoon some of the crumb mixture into each peach half.

5. Bake 1 hour or until the peaches are tender. Serve hot or at room temperature.

Pears in Orange Sauce

Pere all' Arancia

Makes 4 servings

When I visited Anna Tasca Lanza at Regaleali, her family's wine estate in Sicily, she gave me some of her excellent mandarin orange marmalade to take home. Anna uses the marmalade both as a spread and as a dessert sauce, and inspired me to stir some into the poaching liquid of some pears I was cooking. The pears had a beautiful golden glaze, and everyone loved the result. Now I make this dessert often. Because I quickly used up the supply of marmalade Anna gave me, I use quality store-bought orange marmalade.

½ cup sugar

1 cup dry white wine

4 firm ripe pears, such as Anjou, Bartlett, or Bosc

⅓ cup orange marmalade

2 tablespoons orange liqueur or rum

1. In a saucepan just large enough to hold the pears upright, combine the sugar and wine. Over medium heat, bring to a simmer and cook until the sugar is dissolved.

2. Add the pears. Cover the pan and cook about 30 minutes or until the pears are tender when pierced with a knife.

3. With a slotted spoon, transfer the pears to a serving platter. Add the marmalade to the liquid in the saucepan. Bring to a simmer and cook 1 minute. Remove from the heat and stir in the liqueur. Spoon the sauce over and around the pears. Cover and chill in the refrigerator at least 1 hour before serving.

Pears with Marsala and Cream

Pere al Marsala

Makes 4 servings

I had pears prepared this way at a trattoria in Bologna. If you prepare them just before eating dinner, they will be at the right serving temperature when you are ready for dessert.

You can find both dry and sweet Marsala imported from Sicily, though the dry is of better quality. Either can be used for making desserts.

4 large Anjou, Bartlett, or Bosc pears, not too ripe

¼ cup sugar

½ cup water

½ cup dry or sweet Marsala

¼ cup heavy cream

1. Peel the pears and cut them in half lengthwise.

2. In a skillet large enough to hold the pear halves in a single layer, bring the sugar and water to a simmer over medium heat. Stir to

dissolve the sugar. Add the pears and cover the skillet. Cook 5 to 10 minutes or until the pears are almost tender when pierced with a fork.

3. With a slotted spoon, transfer the pears to a plate. Add the Marsala to the skillet and bring to a simmer. Cook until the syrup is slightly thickened, about 5 minutes. Stir in the cream and simmer 2 minutes more.

4. Return the pears to the skillet and baste them with the sauce. Transfer the pears to serving dishes and spoon the sauce over the top. Let cool to room temperature before serving.

Pears with Warm Chocolate Sauce

Pere Affogato al Cioccolato

Makes 6 servings

Sweet fresh pears bathed in a bittersweet chocolate sauce is a classic European dessert. I had this in Bologna, where the chocolate sauce was made with Majani chocolate, a locally made brand that unfortunately does not travel far from its hometown. Use a good-quality bittersweet chocolate. One brand that I like, Scharffen Berger, is made in California.

6 Anjou, Bartlett, or Bosc pears, not too ripe

2 cups water

¾ cup sugar

4 (2 × ½–inch) strips orange zest, cut into matchsticks

1½ cups Warm Chocolate Sauce

1. Peel the pears, leaving the stems intact. With a melon baller or small spoon, scoop out the core and seeds, working from the bottom of the pears.

2. In a saucepan large enough to hold all the pears upright, bring the water, sugar, and orange zest to a simmer over medium heat. Stir until the sugar is dissolved.

3. Add the pears and reduce the heat to low. Cover the pan and cook, turning the pears once, for 20 minutes or until tender when pierced with a small knife. Let the pears cool in the syrup.

4. When ready to serve, prepare the chocolate sauce.

5. With a slotted spoon, transfer the pears to serving dishes. (Cover and refrigerate the syrup for another use, such as tossing with cut-up fruits for a salad.) Drizzle with warm chocolate sauce. Serve immediately.

Rum-Spiced Pears

Pere al Rhum

Makes 6 servings

The sweet, mild, almost floral taste of ripe pears lends itself to many other complementary flavors. Fruits such as oranges, lemons, and berries and many cheeses go well with them, and Marsala and dry wines are often used to poach pears. In Piedmont I was pleasantly surprised to be served these pears simmered in a spiced rum syrup accompanying a simple hazelnut cake.

6 Anjou, Bartlett, or Bosc pears, not too ripe

¼ cup brown sugar

¼ cup dark rum

¼ cup water

4 whole cloves

1. Peel the pears, leaving the stems intact. With a melon baller or small spoon, scoop out the core and seeds, working from the bottom of the pears.

2. In a saucepan just large enough to hold the pears, stir together the sugar, rum, and water over medium heat until the sugar is melted, about 5 minutes. Add the pears. Scatter the cloves around the fruit.

3. Cover the pan and bring the liquid to a simmer. Cook over medium-low heat 15 to 20 minutes or until the pears are tender when pierced with a knife. With a slotted spoon, transfer the pears to a serving dish.

4. Simmer the liquid uncovered until reduced and syrupy. Strain the liquid over the pears. Let cool.

5. Serve at room temperature or cover and chill in the refrigerator.

Spiced Pears with Pecorino

Pere allo Spezie e Pecorino

Makes 6 servings

Tuscans are rightly proud of their excellent sheep's milk cheese. Every town has its own version, and each tastes slightly different from the others, depending on how it is aged and where the milk comes from. Usually the cheeses are eaten when they are quite young and still semifirm. When eaten for dessert, the cheese is sometimes drizzled with a little honey or served with pears. I like this sophisticated presentation that I had in Montalcino—pecorino served with pears cooked in the local red wine and spices, accompanied by fresh walnuts.

Of course, the pears are also good served plain or with a large spoonful of whipped cream.

6 medium Anjou, Bartlett, or Bosc pears, not too ripe

1 cup dry red wine

½ cup sugar

1 (3-inch) piece cinnamon stick

4 whole cloves

8 ounces Pecorino Toscano, Asiago, or Parmigiano-Reggiano cheese, cut into 6 pieces

12 walnut halves, toasted

1. Place a rack in the center of the oven. Preheat the oven to 450°F. Arrange the pears in a baking dish just large enough to hold them upright.

2. Stir together the wine and sugar until the sugar softens. Pour the mixture over the pears. Scatter the cinnamon and cloves around the pears.

3. Bake the pears, basting them occasionally with the wine, 45 to 60 minutes or until they are tender when pierced with a knife. If the liquid begins to dry up before the pears are done, add a little warm water to the pan.

4. Let the pears cool in the dish, basting them occasionally with the pan juices. (As the juices cool, they thicken and coat the pears with a rich red glaze.) Remove the spices.

5. Serve the pears with the syrup at room temperature or slightly chilled. Place them on serving dishes with two walnut halves and a piece of the cheese.

Poached Pears with Gorgonzola

Pere al Gorgonzola

Makes 4 servings

The spicy flavor of gorgonzola cheese blended to a smooth cream is a savory complement to these pears poached in a lemony white-wine syrup. A sprinkling of pistachios adds a bright touch of color. Anjou, Bartlett, and Bosc pears are my favorite varieties for poaching, because their slender shape allows them to cook through evenly. Poached pears hold their shape better when the fruit are not too ripe.

2 cups dry white wine

2 tablespoons fresh lemon juice

¾ cup sugar

2 (2-inch) strips lemon zest

4 pears, such as Anjou, Bartlett, or Bosc

4 ounces gorgonzola

2 tablespoons ricotta, mascarpone, or heavy cream

2 tablespoons chopped pistachios

1. In a medium saucepan, combine the wine, lemon juice, sugar, and lemon zest. Bring to a simmer and cook for 10 minutes.

2. Meanwhile, peel the pears and cut them in half lengthwise. Remove the cores.

3. Slip the pears into the wine syrup and cook until tender when pierced with a knife, about 10 minutes. Let cool.

4. With a slotted spoon, transfer two pear halves to each serving dish, cored-side up. Drizzle the syrup around the pears.

5. In a small bowl, mash the gorgonzola with the ricotta to make a smooth paste. Scoop some of the cheese mixture into the cored space of each pear half. Sprinkle with the pistachios. Serve immediately.

Pear or Apple Pudding Cake

Budino di Pere o Mele

Makes 6 servings

Not quite a cake or a pudding, this dessert consists of fruit cooked until tender, then baked with a slightly cakelike topping. It is good with apples or pears or even peaches or plums.

I like to use dark rum for flavoring this dessert, but light rum, cognac, or even grappa can be substituted.

¾ cup raisins

½ cup dark rum, cognac, or grappa

2 tablespoons unsalted butter

8 firm ripe pears or apples, peeled and cut into ½-inch slices

⅓ cup sugar

Topping

6 tablespoons unsalted butter, melted and cooled

⅓ cup sugar

½ cup all-purpose flour

3 large eggs, separated

⅔ cup whole milk

2 tablespoons dark rum, cognac, or grappa

1 teaspoon pure vanilla extract

Pinch of salt

Confectioner's sugar

1. In a small bowl, toss together the raisins and rum. Let stand for 30 minutes.

2. Melt the butter in a large skillet over medium heat. Add the fruit and sugar. Cook, stirring occasionally, until the fruit is almost tender, about 7 minutes. Add the raisins and rum. Cook 2 minutes more. Remove from the heat.

3. Place a rack in the center of the oven. Preheat the oven to 350°F. Grease a 13 × 9 × 2–inch baking dish. Spoon the fruit mixture into the baking dish.

4. Prepare the topping: In a large bowl, with an electric mixer, beat the butter and sugar until blended, about 3 minutes. Stir in the flour, just to combine.

5. In a medium bowl, whisk together the egg yolks, milk, rum, and vanilla. Stir the egg mixture into the flour mixture until blended.

6. In another large bowl, with clean beaters beat the egg whites with the salt on low speed until foamy. Increase the speed and beat until soft peaks form, about 4 minutes. Gently fold the whites into the rest of the batter. Pour the batter over the fruit in the baking dish and bake 25 minutes or until the top is golden and firm to the touch.

7. Serve warm or at room temperature, sprinkled with confectioner's sugar.

Warm Fruit Compote

Composta di Frutta Calda

Makes 6 to 8 servings

Rum is often used to flavor desserts in Italy. Dark rum has a deeper flavor than light rum. Substitute another liqueur or a sweet wine such as Marsala for the rum in this recipe if you like. Or make a nonalcoholic version with orange or apple juice.

2 firm ripe pears, peeled and cored

1 golden delicious or Granny Smith apple, peeled and cored

1 cup pitted prunes

1 cup dried figs, stem ends removed

½ cup dried pitted apricots

½ cup dark raisins

¼ cup sugar

2 (2-inch) strips lemon zest

1 cup water

½ cup dark rum

1. Cut the pears and apple into 8 wedges. Cut the wedges into bite-size pieces.

2. Combine all of the ingredients in a large saucepan. Cover and bring to a simmer over medium-low heat. Cook until the fresh fruits are tender and the dried fruits are plump, about 20 minutes. Add a little more water if they seem dry.

3. Let cool slightly before serving or cover and refrigerate up to 3 days.

Venetian Caramelized Fruit

Golosezzi Veneziani

Makes 8 servings

The caramel coating on these Venetian skewered fruits hardens, with a result something like a candy apple. Pat the fruits thoroughly dry and make these fruit skewers on a dry day. If the weather is humid, the caramel will not harden properly.

1 tangerine or clementine, peeled, divided into sections

8 small strawberries, hulled

8 seedless grapes

8 pitted dates

1 cup sugar

½ cup light corn syrup

¼ cup water

1. Thread the fruit pieces alternately on each of eight 6-inch wood skewers. Set a wire cooling rack on top of a tray.

2. In a skillet large enough to fit the skewers into lengthwise, combine the sugar, corn syrup, and water. Cook over medium heat, stirring occasionally until the sugar is completely dissolved, about 3 minutes. When the mixture begins to boil, stop stirring and cook until the syrup starts to brown around the edges. Then gently swirl the pan over the heat until the syrup is an even golden brown, about 2 minutes more.

3. Remove the pan from the heat. Using tongs, quickly dip each skewer in the syrup, turning to coat the fruit lightly but thoroughly. Let the excess syrup drain back into the pan. Place the skewers on the rack to cool. (If the syrup in the pan hardens before all of the skewers have been dipped, reheat it gently.) Serve at room temperature within 2 hours.

Fruit with Honey and Grappa

Composta di Frutta alla Grappa

Makes 6 servings

Grappa is a kind of brandy made from vinaccia, the skins and seeds that are left after grapes are pressed to make wine. At one time, grappa was a coarse beverage mostly drunk in northern Italy by farmhands and laborers for warmth on cold winter days. Today, grappa is a very refined drink, sold in designer bottles with ornate stoppers. Some grappas are flavored with fruit or herbs, while others are aged in wood casks. Use a simple, unflavored grappa for this fruit salad and for other cooking purposes.

⅓ cup honey

⅓ cup grappa, brandy, or fruit liqueur

1 tablespoon fresh lemon juice

2 kiwis, peeled and sliced

2 navel oranges, peeled and cut into wedges

1 pint strawberries, sliced

1 cup halved seedless green grapes

2 medium bananas, sliced

1. In a large serving bowl, mix together the honey, grappa, and lemon juice.

2. Stir in the kiwis, oranges, strawberries, and grapes. Chill for at least 1 hour or up to 4 hours. Stir in the bananas just before serving.

Winter Fruit Salad

Macedonia del' Inverno

Makes 6 servings

In Italy, a fruit salad is called Macedonia, because that country was once divided up into many little sections that were brought together to make a whole, just as the salad is made up of bite-size pieces of different fruits. In the winter, when fruit choices are limited, Italians make salads like this one dressed with honey and lemon juice. As a variation, substitute apricot jam or orange marmalade for the honey.

3 tablespoons honey

3 tablespoons orange juice

1 tablespoon fresh lemon juice

2 grapefruits, peeled and separated into wedges

2 kiwis, peeled and sliced

2 ripe pears

2 cups seedless green grapes, halved lengthwise

1. In a large bowl, mix together the honey, orange juice, and lemon juice.

2. Add the fruits to the bowl and toss well. Chill for at least 1 hour or up to 4 hours before serving.

Grilled Summer Fruit

Spiedini alla Frutta

Makes 6 servings

Grilled summer fruits are great for a barbecue. Serve them plain or with slices of sponge cake and ice cream.

If using wood skewers, soak them in cold water at least 30 minutes to prevent burning.

2 nectarines, cut into 1-inch chunks

2 plums, cut into 1-inch chunks

2 pears, cut into 1-inch chunks

2 apricots, cut into quarters

2 bananas, cut into 1-inch chunks

Fresh mint leaves

About 2 tablespoons sugar

1. Place a barbecue grill or broiler rack about 5 inches away from the heat source. Preheat the grill or broiler.

2. Alternate pieces of the fruits with the mint leaves on 6 skewers. Sprinkle with the sugar.

3. Grill or broil the fruit 3 minutes on one side. Turn the skewers and grill or broil until lightly browned, about 2 minutes more. Serve hot.

Warm Ricotta with Honey

Ricotta al Miele

Makes 2 to 3 servings

The success of this dessert depends on the quality of the ricotta, so buy the freshest available. While part-skimmed-milk ricotta is fine, the fat-free is very grainy and tasteless, so don't use it. If you like, add some fresh fruit, or try raisins and a pinch of cinnamon.

1 cup whole-milk ricotta

2 tablespoons honey

1. Place the ricotta in a small bowl set over a smaller pan of simmering water. Heat until warm, about 10 minutes. Stir well.

2. Scoop the ricotta into serving dishes. Drizzle with the honey. Serve immediately.

Coffee Ricotta

Ricotta all' Caffè

Makes 2 to 3 servings

Here is a quick dessert that lends itself to a multitude of variations. Serve it with some plain butter cookies.

If you can't buy finely ground espresso, be sure to run the grounds through your coffee grinder or food processor. If the grounds are too large, the dessert won't blend right, leaving it with a gritty texture.

1 cup (8 ounces) whole or part-skim ricotta

1 tablespoon finely ground (espresso) coffee

1 tablespoon sugar

Chocolate shavings

> In a medium bowl, whisk together the ricotta, espresso, and sugar until the mixture is smooth and the sugar is dissolved. (For a creamier texture, mix the ingredients in a food processor.) Spoon into parfait glasses or goblets and top with chocolate shavings. Serve immediately.

Variation: For chocolate ricotta, substitute 1 tablespoon unsweetened cocoa for the coffee.

Mascarpone and Peaches

Mascarpone al Pesche

Makes 6 servings

Smooth, creamy mascarpone and peaches with crunchy amaretti look beautiful in parfait or wine glasses. Serve this dessert at a dinner party. No one will guess how easy it is to make.

1 cup (8 ounces) mascarpone

¼ cup sugar

1 tablespoon fresh lemon juice

1 cup very cold whipping cream

3 peaches or nectarines, peeled and cut into bite-size pieces

⅓ cup orange liqueur, amaretto, or rum

8 amaretti cookies, crushed into crumbs (about ½ cup)

2 tablespoons toasted sliced almonds

1. At least 20 minutes before you are ready to make the dessert, place a large bowl and the beaters of an electric mixer in the refrigerator.

2. When ready, in a medium bowl, whisk together the mascarpone, sugar, and lemon juice. Remove the bowl and beaters from the refrigerator. Pour the cream into the chilled bowl and whip the cream at high speed until it holds its shape softly when the beaters are lifted, about 4 minutes. With a spatula, gently fold the whipped cream into the mascarpone mixture.

3. In a medium bowl, toss together the peaches and liqueur.

4. Spoon half of the mascarpone cream into six parfait glasses or wine goblets. Make a layer of the peaches, then sprinkle with the amaretti crumbs. Top with the remaining cream. Cover and chill in the refrigerator up to 2 hours.

5. Sprinkle with the almonds before serving.

Chocolate Foam with Raspberries

Spuma di Cioccolato al Lampone

Makes 8 servings

Whipped cream folded into mascarpone and chocolate is like an instant chocolate mousse. The raspberries are a sweet and tangy complement.

1 pint raspberries

1 to 2 tablespoons sugar

2 tablespoons raspberry, cherry, or orange liqueur

3 ounces bittersweet or semisweet chocolate

½ cup (4 ounces) mascarpone, at room temperature

2 cups chilled heavy or whipping cream

Chocolate shavings, for garnish

1. At least 20 minutes before you are ready to make the dessert, place a large bowl and the beaters of an electric mixer in the refrigerator.

2. When ready, toss the raspberries with the sugar and liqueur in a medium bowl. Set aside.

3. Fill a small pot with an inch of water. Bring it to a simmer over low heat. Place the chocolate in a bowl larger than the rim of the pot and set the bowl over the simmering water. Let stand until the chocolate is melted. Remove from the heat and stir the chocolate until smooth. Let cool slightly, about 15 minutes. With a rubber spatula, fold in the mascarpone.

4. Remove the chilled bowl and beaters from the refrigerator. Pour the cream into the bowl and whip the cream at high speed until it holds its shape softly when the beaters are lifted, about 4 minutes.

5. With a spatula, gently fold half of the cream into the chocolate mixture, reserving the second half for the topping.

6. Spoon half of the chocolate cream into eight parfait glasses. Layer with the raspberries. Spoon on the remaining chocolate cream. Top with the whipped cream. Garnish with the chocolate shavings. Serve immediately.

Tiramisù

Tiramisù

Makes 8 to 10 servings

No one is quite sure why this dessert is called "pick me up" in Italian, but it is assumed the name comes from the jolt of caffeine it provides from the coffee and chocolate. While the classic version contains raw egg yolks mixed in with the mascarpone, my version is eggless because I do not like the flavor of raw eggs and find they make the dessert heavier than it needs to be.

Savoiardi—crisp ladyfingers imported from Italy—are widely available, but ordinary lady fingers or slices of plain cake can be substituted. If you like, add a couple of tablespoons of rum or cognac to the coffee.

1 cup chilled heavy or whipping cream

1 pound mascarpone

⅓ cup sugar

24 savoiardi (imported Italian ladyfingers)

1 cup brewed espresso coffee at room temperature

2 tablespoons unsweetened cocoa powder

1. At least 20 minutes before you are ready to make the dessert, place a large bowl and the beaters of an electric mixer in the refrigerator.

2. When ready, remove the bowl and beaters from the refrigerator. Pour the cream into the bowl and whip the cream at high speed until it holds its shape softly when the beaters are lifted, about 4 minutes.

3. In a large bowl, whisk together the mascarpone and sugar until smooth. Take about one third of the whipped cream, and with a flexible spatula, gently fold it into the mascarpone mixture to lighten it. Carefully fold in the remaining cream.

4. Lightly and quickly dip half of the savoiardi in the coffee. (Do not saturate them or they will fall apart.) Arrange the cookies in a single layer in a 9 × 2–inch square or round serving dish. Spoon on half of the mascarpone cream.

5. Dip the remaining savoiardi in the coffee and arrange them in a layer over the mascarpone. Top with the remaining mascarpone mixture and spread it smooth with the spatula. Place the cocoa in a fine-mesh strainer and shake it over the top of the dessert. Cover with foil or plastic wrap and refrigerate 3 to 4 hours or

overnight so that the flavors can meld. It will keep well in the refrigerator up to 24 hours.

Strawberry Tiramisù

Tiramisù alle Fragole

Makes 8 servings

Here is a strawberry version of tiramisù that I came across in an Italian cooking magazine. I like it even better than the coffee version, but then I favor fruit-based desserts of all kinds.

Maraschino is a clear, slightly bitter Italian cherry liqueur named for the marasche variety of cherries. Maraschino is available here, but you can substitute another fruit liqueur if you prefer.

3 pints strawberries, washed and hulled

½ cup orange juice

¼ cup maraschino, crème di cassis, or orange liqueur

¼ cup sugar

1 cup chilled heavy or whipping cream

8 ounces mascarpone

24 savoiardi (Italian lady fingers)

1. Set aside 2 cups of the best-looking strawberries for garnish. Chop the remainder. In a large bowl, combine the strawberries with the orange juice, liqueur, and sugar. Let stand at room temperature 1 hour.

2. Meanwhile, place a large bowl and the beaters of an electric mixer in the refrigerator. When ready, remove the bowl and beaters from the refrigerator. Pour the cream into the bowl and whip the cream at high speed until it holds its shape softly when the beaters are lifted, about 4 minutes. With a flexible spatula, gently fold in the mascarpone.

3. Make a layer of ladyfingers in a 9 × 2–inch square or round serving dish. Spoon on half of the strawberries and their juice. Spread half of the mascarpone cream over the berries.

4. Repeat with a second layer of ladyfingers, strawberries, and cream, spreading the cream smooth with a spatula. Cover and refrigerate 3 to 4 hours or overnight so that the flavors can meld.

5. Just before serving, slice the remaining strawberries and arrange them in rows on top.

Italian Trifle

Zuppa Inglese

Makes 10 to 12 servings

"English soup" is the whimsical name for this lush dessert. It is believed that Italian cooks borrowed the idea from English trifle and added Italian touches.

1 Vin Santo Rings or 1 (12-ounce) store-bought pound cake, cut into slices, 1/4 inch thick

1/2 cup sour cherry or raspberrry jam

1/2 cup dark rum or orange liqueur

2 1/2 cups each Chocolate and Vanilla Pastry Cream

1 cup heavy or whipping cream

Fresh raspberries, for garnish

Chocolate shavings, for garnish

1. Prepare the sponge cake and pastry creams, if necessary. Then, in a small bowl, stir together the jam and rum.

2. Spoon half of the vanilla pastry cream into the bottom of a 3-quart serving bowl. Place $1/4$ of the cake slices on top and brush with $1/4$ of the jam mixture. Spoon half of the chocolate pastry cream on top.

3. Make another layer of $1/4$ of the cake and jam mixture. Repeat with the remaining vanilla cream, $1/4$ of the remaining cake and jam mixture, chocolate cream, and the rest of the cake and jam mixture. Cover tightly with plastic and refrigerate at least 3 hours and up to 24 hours.

4. At least 20 minutes before serving, place a large bowl and the beaters of an electric mixer in the refrigerator. Just before serving, remove the bowl and beaters from the refrigerator. Pour the cream into the bowl and whip at high speed until it holds its shape softly when the beaters are lifted, about 4 minutes.

5. Spoon the cream on top of the trifle. Garnish with raspberries and chocolate shavings.

Zabaglione

Makes 2 servings

In Italy, zabaglione (pronounced tsah-bahl-yo-neh; the g is silent) is a sweet, creamy, egg-based dessert, often served as a strength-building tonic for someone suffering from a cold or other ailment. Illness or no illness, it is a delicious dessert on its own or as a sauce for fruit or cake.

Zabaglione should be eaten as soon as it is made, or it can collapse. To make zabaglione ahead of time, see the recipe for chilled zabaglione.

3 large egg yolks

3 tablespoons sugar

3 tablespoons dry or sweet Marsala or vin santo

1. In the bottom half of a double boiler or in a medium saucepan, bring about 2 inches of water to a simmer.

2. In the top half of the double boiler or in a heatproof bowl that fits comfortably over the saucepan, beat the egg yolks and sugar with a hand-held electric mixer on medium speed until light, about 2 minutes. Blend in the Marsala. Place the mixture over the simmering water. (Do not allow the water to boil, or the eggs will scramble.)

3. While it warms over the simmering water, continue to beat the egg mixture until it is pale yellow and very fluffy and holds a soft shape when dropped from the beaters, 3 to 5 minutes.

4. Spoon into tall goblets and serve immediately.

Chocolate Zabaglione

Zabaglione al Cioccolato

Makes 4 servings

This variation on zabaglione is like a rich chocolate mousse. Serve it warm with cool whipped cream.

3 ounces bittersweet or semisweet chocolate, chopped

¼ cup heavy cream

4 large egg yolks

¼ cup sugar

2 tablespoons rum or amaretto liqueur

1. In the bottom half of a double boiler or in a medium saucepan, bring about 2 inches of water to a simmer. Combine the chocolate and cream in a small heatproof bowl set over the simmering water. Let stand until the chocolate is melted. Stir with a flexible spatula until smooth. Remove from the heat.

2. In the top of the double boiler or in another heatproof bowl that fits over the saucepan, beat the egg yolks and sugar with a hand-

held electric mixer until light, about 2 minutes. Blend in the rum. Place the mixture over the simmering water. (Do not allow the water to boil, or the eggs will scramble.)

3. Beat the yolk mixture until it is pale and fluffy and holds a soft shape when dropped from the beaters, 3 to 5 minutes. Remove from the heat.

4. With a rubber spatula, gently fold in the chocolate mixture. Serve immediately.

Chilled Zabaglione with Berries

Zabaglione Freddo con Frutti di Bosco

Makes 6 servings

If you don't want to make zabaglione right before serving, this cold version is a good alternative. The zabaglione is cooled in an ice-water bath, then folded into whipped cream. It can be made up to 24 hours ahead. I like to serve it over fresh berries or ripe figs.

1 recipe (about 1½ cups) Zabaglione

¾ cup chilled heavy or whipping cream

2 tablespoons confectioner's sugar

1 tablespoon orange liqueur

1½ cups blueberries, raspberries, or a combination, rinsed and patted dry

1. At least 20 minutes before you are ready to make the zabaglione, place a large bowl and the beaters of an electric mixer in the refrigerator. Fill another large bowl with ice and water.

2. Prepare the zabaglione through step 3. As soon as the zabaglione is finished, remove it from the simmering water and set the bowl over the ice water. With a wire whisk, beat the zabaglione until it is cold, about 3 minutes.

3. Remove the chilled bowl and beaters from the refrigerator. Pour the cream into the bowl and whip the cream at high speed until it begins to hold a soft shape, about 2 minutes. Add the confectioner's sugar and orange liqueur. Whip the cream until it holds a soft shape when the beaters are lifted, about 2 minutes more. With a flexible spatula, gently fold in the chilled zabaglione. Cover and chill in the refrigerator at least 1 hour until ready to serve.

4. Divide the berries among 6 serving dishes. Top with the chilled zabaglione cream and serve immediately.

Lemon Gelatin

Gelatina di Limone

Makes 6 servings

Lemon juice and zest make this dessert light and refreshing.

2 envelopes unflavored gelatin

1 cup sugar

2½ cups cold water

2 (2-inch) strips lemon zest

⅔ cup fresh lemon juice

Lemon slices and mint sprigs, for garnish

1. In a medium saucepan, stir together the gelatin and sugar. Add the water and lemon zest. Cook over medium heat, stirring constantly, until the gelatin is completely dissolved, about 3 minutes. (Do not allow the mixture to boil.)

2. Remove from the heat and stir in the lemon juice. Pour the mixture through a fine-mesh strainer into a 5-cup mold or bowl. Cover and chill until set, 4 hours up to overnight.

3. When ready to serve, fill a bowl with warm water and dip the mold into the water for 30 seconds. Run a small knife around the sides. Lay a plate over the mold, and holding them together, invert them both so that the gelatin transfers to the plate. Garnish with lemon slices and mint sprigs.

Orange Rum Gelatin

Gelatina di Arancia al Rhum

Makes 4 servings

Rum-scented whipped cream is a nice accompaniment. Blood orange juice works best here.

2 envelopes unflavored gelatin

½ cup sugar

½ cup cold water

3 cups fresh orange juice

2 tablespoons dark rum

Orange slices, for garnish

1. In a medium saucepan, stir together the gelatin and sugar. Add the water and cook over medium heat, stirring constantly, until the gelatin is completely dissolved, about 3 minutes. (Do not allow the mixture to boil.)

2. Remove from the heat and stir in orange juice and rum. Pour mixture into a 5-cup mold or bowl. Cover and chill until set, 4 hours up to overnight.

3. When ready to serve, fill a bowl with warm water and dip the mold into the water for 30 seconds. Run a small knife around the sides. Lay a plate over the mold, and holding them together, invert them both so that the gelatin transfers to the plate. Garnish with the orange slices.

Espresso Gelatin

Gelatina di Caffè

Makes 4 servings

When I first tasted this coffee gelatin in Milan, it was served with both whipped cream and Chilled Zabaglione, a dazzling combination. This is also refreshing, light, and delicious on its own.

2 envelopes unflavored gelatin

1 cup sugar

2½ cup cold water

2 tablespoons instant espresso powder

1. In a medium saucepan, stir together the gelatin and sugar. Add the water and cook over medium heat, stirring constantly, until the gelatin is completely dissolved, about 3 minutes. Do not allow the mixture to boil.

2. Remove from the heat. Stir in the instant coffee. Pour the mixture into a 1-quart mold. Cover and chill until set, 4 hours up to overnight.

3. When ready to serve, fill a bowl with warm water and dip the mold into the water for 30 seconds. Run a small knife around the sides. Lay a plate over the mold, and holding them together, invert them so the gelatin transfers to the plate.

Panna Cotta

Makes 6 servings

The best version of this dessert I have had was in Piedmont at the Giardino da Felicin, a favorite restaurant in Monforte d'Alba. It had just been made and was barely gelled. When I touched it with my spoon, its shape yielded smoothly. The dessert melted in my mouth and tasted of nothing but the finest sweet, fresh cream.

The name of this Piedmontese dessert means "cooked cream," though there is practically no cooking involved. A fresh berry sauce or warm chocolate sauce goes well with it, or just some fresh fruit.

1 envelope unflavored gelatin

1½ cups whole milk

1½ cups heavy or whipping cream

1 vanilla bean or 2 teaspoons pure vanilla extract

1 (2-inch) strip lemon zest

¼ cup sugar

> Fresh Strawberry Sauce

1. Sprinkle the gelatin over the milk and let stand 2 minutes until the gelatin absorbs some of the liquid and softens.

2. In a medium saucepan, combine the cream, vanilla bean (if using vanilla extract, reserve until later), lemon zest, and sugar. Bring to a simmer over medium heat. Add the gelatin mixture and cook, stirring frequently, until the gelatin is completely dissolved, about 3 minutes.

3. Remove the vanilla bean and lemon zest with a slotted spoon. Slit the vanilla bean lengthwise with a small sharp knife and scrape the seeds out. Stir the seeds into the cream mixture. (Or add the vanilla extract, if using.)

4. Pour the cream into a large bowl. Fill a larger bowl with ice and set the bowl with the cream in the ice. Let the cream cool, stirring frequently, until it begins to set, about 10 minutes. Pour the cream into 6 individual custard cups. Cover and chill until set, 4 hours up to overnight.

5. Prepare the strawberry sauce, if necessary. When ready to serve, briefly dip the bottom of the cups in a bowl filled with warm water to loosen. Run a small knife around the inside of the cups. Invert the cups onto serving plates. Spoon the sauce over each and serve.

Butter Rings

Bussolai

Makes 36

These Venetian cookies are simple to make and a pleasure to have around the house for a midday snack or whenever guests stop in.

1 cup sugar

½ cup (1 stick) unsalted butter, at room temperature

3 large egg yolks

1 teaspoon grated lemon zest

1 teaspoon grated orange zest

1 teaspoon pure vanilla extract

2 cups all-purpose flour

½ teaspoon salt

1 egg white, beaten until foamy

1. Set aside $1/3$ cup of the sugar.

2. In the large bowl of an electric mixer, beat the butter with the remaining ⅔ cup of sugar at medium speed until light and fluffy, about 2 minutes. Beat in the egg yolks one at a time. Add the lemon and orange zests and vanilla extract and beat, scraping the sides of the bowl, until smooth, about 2 minutes more.

3. Stir in the flour and salt until well blended. Shape the dough into a ball. Wrap in plastic wrap and refrigerate 1 hour up to overnight.

4. Preheat the oven to 325°F. Grease 2 large baking sheets. Cut the dough into 6 pieces. Divide each piece again into 6 pieces. Roll each piece into a 4-inch rope, shape into a ring, and pinch the ends together to seal. Place the rings 1 inch apart on the prepared baking sheets. Brush lightly with the egg white and sprinkle with the reserved ⅓ cup of sugar.

5. Bake 15 minutes or until lightly browned. Have ready 2 wire cooling racks.

6. Transfer the baking sheets to the racks. Let the cookies cool 5 minutes on the baking sheets, then transfer them to the wire racks to cool completely. Store in an airtight container up to 2 weeks.

Lemon Knots

Tarralucci

Makes 40

Every Italian bakery in Brooklyn, New York, made these refreshing Sicilian lemon cookies when I was growing up. I like to serve them with iced tea.

If the weather is hot and humid, the icing may refuse to firm up at room temperature. In that case, store the cookies in the refrigerator.

4 cups all-purpose flour

4 teaspoons baking powder

1 cup sugar

½ cup solid vegetable shortening

3 large eggs

½ cup milk

2 tablespoons lemon juice

2 teaspoons grated lemon zest

Icing

1½ cups confectioner's sugar

1 tablespoon freshly squeezed lemon juice

2 teaspoons grated lemon zest

Milk

1. Sift together the flour and baking powder onto a piece of wax paper.

2. In a large bowl, with an electric mixer at medium speed, beat the sugar and shortening until light and fluffy, about 2 minutes. Beat in the eggs one at a time until well blended. Stir in the milk, lemon juice, and zest. Scrape the sides of the bowl. Stir in the dry ingredients until smooth, about 2 minutes. Cover with plastic wrap and refrigerate at least 1 hour.

3. Preheat the oven to 350°F. Have ready 2 large baking sheets. Pinch off a piece of dough the size of a golf ball. Lightly roll the dough into a 6-inch rope. Tie the rope into a knot. Place the knot on an ungreased baking sheet. Continue making the knots and placing them about 1 inch apart on the sheets.

4. Bake the cookies 12 minutes or until firm when pressed on top but not browned. Have ready 2 wire cooling racks.

5. Transfer the baking sheets to the racks. Let the cookies cool 5 minutes on the baking sheets, then transfer them to the wire racks to cool completely.

6. Combine the confectioner's sugar, lemon juice, and zest in a large bowl. Add milk 1 teaspoon at a time and stir until the mixture forms a thin icing with the consistency of heavy cream.

7. Dip the tops of the cookies in the icing. Place them on a rack until the icing is hardened. Store in airtight containers up to 3 days.

Spice Cookies

Bicciolani

Makes 75

In caffès in Turin you can order barbajada, a combination of half coffee and half hot chocolate. It would be perfect with these thin, buttery spice cookies.

1 cup (2 sticks) unsalted butter, at room temperature

1 cup sugar

1 egg yolk

2 cups all-purpose flour

½ teaspoon salt

1 teaspoon ground cinnamon

⅛ teaspoon freshly grated nutmeg

⅛ teaspoon ground cloves

1. Preheat the oven to 350°F. Grease a 15 × 10 × 1– inch jelly roll pan.

2. In a bowl, stir together the flour, salt, and spices.

3. In a large electric mixer bowl, beat the butter, sugar, and egg yolk on medium speed until light and fluffy, about 2 minutes. Reduce the speed to low and stir in the dry ingredients until thoroughly blended, about 2 minutes more.

4. Crumble the dough into the prepared pan. With your hands, firmly press the dough out into an even layer. With the back of a fork, make shallow ridges in the top of the dough.

5. Bake 25 to 30 minutes or until lightly browned. Transfer the pan to a wire cooling rack. Cool 10 minutes. Then cut the dough into 2 × 1-inch cookies.

6. Cool completely in the pan. Store at room temperature in an airtight container up to 2 weeks.

Wafer Cookies

Pizzelle

Makes about 2 dozen

Many families in central and southern Italy are proud of their pizzelle irons, beautifully crafted forms traditionally used to make these pretty wafers. Some irons are embossed with the original owner's initials, while others have silhouettes such as a couple toasting each other with a glass of wine. They were once a typical wedding gift.

Though charming, these old fashioned irons are heavy and unwieldy on today's stoves. An electric pizzelle press, similar to a waffle iron, does an efficient and quick job of turning out these cookies.

When they are freshly made, pizzelle are pliable and can be molded into cone, tube, or cup shapes. They can be filled with whipped cream, ice cream, cannoli cream, or fruit. They cool and crisp in no time, so you must work quickly and carefully to shape them. Of course, they are good flat as well.

1¾ cups unbleached all-purpose flour

1 teaspoon baking powder

Pinch of salt

3 large eggs

⅔ cup sugar

1 tablespoon pure vanilla extract

1 stick (½ cup) unsalted butter, melted and cooled

1. Preheat the pizzelle maker according to the manufacturer's directions. In a bowl, stir together the flour, baking powder, and salt.

2. In a large bowl, beat the eggs, sugar, and vanilla with an electric mixer on medium speed until thick and light, about 4 minutes. Beat in the butter. Stir in the dry ingredients until just blended, about 1 minute.

3. Place about 1 tablespoon of the batter in the center of each pizzelle mold. (The exact amount will depend on the design of the mold.) Close the cover and bake until lightly golden. This will depend on the maker and how long the mold has been heating. Check it carefully after 30 seconds.

4. When the pizzelle are golden, slide them off the molds with a wooden or plastic spatula. Let cool flat on a wire rack. Or, to

make cookie cups, bend each pizzelle into the curve of a wide coffee or dessert cup. To make cannoli shells, shape them around cannoli tubes or a wooden dowel.

5. When the pizzelle are cool and crisp, store them in an airtight container until ready to use. These last for several weeks.

Variation: *Anise*: Substitute 1 tablespoon anise extract and 1 tablespoon anise seeds for the vanilla. *Orange or Lemon*: Add 1 tablespoon grated fresh orange or lemon zest to the egg mixture. *Rum or Almond*: Stir in 1 tablespoon rum or almond extract instead of the vanilla. *Nut*: Stir in $1/4$ cup of nuts ground to a very fine powder along with the flour.

Sweet Ravioli

Ravioli Dolci

Makes 2 dozen

Jam fills these crisp dessert ravioli. Any flavor will do, as long as it has a thick consistency so that it will stay in place and not ooze out of the dough as it bakes. This was a favorite recipe of my father, who perfected it from his memories of the cookies his mother used to make.

1¾ cup all-purpose flour

½ cup potato or corn starch

½ teaspoon salt

½ cup (1 stick) unsalted butter, at room temperature

½ cup sugar

1 large egg

2 tablespoons rum or brandy

1 teaspoon grated lemon zest

1 teaspoon pure vanilla extract

1 cup thick sour cherry, raspberry, or apricot jam

1. In a large bowl, sift together the flour, starch, and salt.

2. In a large bowl with an electric mixer, beat the butter with the sugar until light and fluffy, about 2 minutes. Beat in the egg, rum, zest, and vanilla. On low speed, stir in the dry ingredients.

3. Divide the dough in half. Shape each half into a disk. Wrap each separately in plastic and refrigerate 1 hour up to overnight.

4. Preheat the oven to 350°F. Grease 2 large baking sheets.

5. Roll out the dough to a $1/8$-inch thickness. With a fluted pastry or pasta cutter, cut the dough into 2-inch squares. Arrange the squares about 1 inch apart on the prepared baking sheets. Place $1/2$ teaspoon of the jam in the center of each square. (Do not use more jam, or the filling will leak out as it bakes.)

6. Roll out the remaining dough to a $1/8$-inch thickness. Cut the dough into 2-inch squares.

7. Cover the jam with the dough squares. Press the edges all around with a fork to seal in the filling.

8. Bake 16 to 18 minutes, or until lightly browned. Have ready 2 wire cooling racks.

9. Transfer the baking sheets to the racks. Let the cookies cool 5 minutes on the baking sheets, then transfer them to the wire racks to cool completely. Sprinkle with confectioner's sugar. Store in an airtight container up to 1 week.

"Ugly-but-Good" Cookies

Brutti ma Buoni

Makes 2 dozen

"Ugly but good" is the meaning of the name of these Piedmontese cookies. The name is only half-true: The cookies are not ugly, but they are good. The technique for making these is unusual. The cookie batter is cooked in a saucepan before it is baked.

3 large egg whites, at room temperature

Pinch of salt

1½ cups sugar

1 cup unsweetened cocoa powder

1¼ cups hazelnuts, toasted, peeled, and coarsely chopped (see How To Toast and Skin Nuts)

1. Preheat the oven to 300°F. Grease 2 large baking sheets.

2. In a large bowl, with an electric mixer at medium speed, beat the egg whites and salt until foamy. Increase the speed to high and gradually add the sugar. Beat until soft peaks form when the beaters are lifted.

3. On low speed, mix in the cocoa. Stir in the hazelnuts.

4. Scrape the mixture into a large heavy saucepan. Cook over medium heat, stirring constantly with a wooden spoon, until the mixture is shiny and smooth, about 5 minutes. Be careful that it does not scorch.

5. Immediately drop the hot batter by tablespoonfuls onto the prepared baking sheets. Bake 30 minutes or until firm and slightly cracked on the surface.

6. While the cookies are still hot, transfer them to a rack to cool, using a thin-blade metal spatula. Store in an airtight container up to 2 weeks.

Jam Spots

Biscotti di Marmellata

Makes 40

Chocolate, nuts, and jam are a winning combination in these tasty cookies. They are always a hit on Christmas cookie trays.

¾ cup (1½ sticks) unsalted butter, at room temperature

½ cup sugar

½ teaspoon salt

3 ounces bittersweet chocolate, melted and cooled

2 cups all-purpose flour

¾ cup finely chopped almonds

½ cup thick seedless raspberry jam

1. Preheat the oven to 350°F. Grease 2 large baking sheets.

2. In a large bowl, with an electric mixer on medium speed, beat the butter, sugar, and salt until light and fluffy, about 2 minutes.

Add the melted chocolate and beat until well blended, scraping the sides of the bowl. Stir in the flour until smooth.

3. Place the nuts in a shallow bowl. Shape the dough into 1-inch balls. Roll the balls in the nuts, pressing lightly so they will adhere. Place the balls about $1^1/_2$ inches apart on the prepared baking sheets.

4. With the handle end of a wooden spoon, poke a deep hole in each ball of dough, molding the dough around the handle to maintain the round shape. Place about $^1/_4$ teaspoon jam in each cookie. (Do not add more jam, as it may melt and leak out when the cookies bake.)

5. Bake the cookies 18 to 20 minutes, or until the jam is bubbling and the cookies are lightly browned. Have ready 2 wire cooling racks.

6. Transfer the baking sheets to the racks. Let the cookies cool 5 minutes on the baking sheets, then transfer them to the wire racks to cool completely. Store in an airtight container up to 2 weeks.

Double-Chocolate Nut Biscotti

Biscotti al Cioccolato

Makes 4 dozen

These rich biscotti have chocolate in the dough, both melted and in chunks. I have never seen them in Italy, but they are similar to what I have tasted in coffee bars here.

2½ cups all-purpose flour

2 teaspoons baking powder

½ teaspoon salt

3 large eggs, at room temperature

1 cup sugar

1 teaspoon pure vanilla extract

6 ounces bittersweet chocolate, melted and cooled

6 tablespoons (½ stick plus 2 tablespoons) unsalted butter, melted and cooled

1 cup walnuts, coarsely chopped

1 cup chocolate chips

1. Place a rack in the center of the oven. Preheat the oven to 300°F. Grease and flour 2 large baking sheets.

2. In a large bowl, sift together the flour, baking powder, and salt.

3. In a large bowl, with an electric mixer at medium speed, beat the eggs, sugar, and vanilla until foamy and light, about 2 minutes. Stir in the chocolate and butter until blended. Add the flour mixture and stir until smooth, about 1 minute more. Stir in the nuts and chocolate chips.

4. Divide the dough in half. With moistened hands, shape each piece into a 12 × 3–inch log on the prepared baking sheet. Bake for 35 minutes or until the logs are firm when pressed in the center. Remove the pan from the oven, but do not turn off the heat. Let cool 10 minutes.

5. Slide the logs onto a cutting board. Cut the logs into $1/2$-inch-thick slices. Lay the slices on the baking sheet. Bake for 10 minutes or until the cookies are lightly toasted.

6. Have ready 2 large cooling racks. Transfer the baking sheets to the racks. Let the cookies cool 5 minutes on the baking sheets,

then transfer them to the racks to cool completely. Store in an airtight container up to 2 weeks.

Chocolate Kisses

Baci di Cioccolato

Makes 3 dozen

Chocolate and vanilla "kisses" are a favorite in Verona, home of Romeo and Juliet, where they are made in a variety of combinations.

1⅔ cups all-purpose flour

⅓ cup unsweetened Dutch-process cocoa powder, sifted

¼ teaspoon salt

1 cup (2 sticks) unsalted butter, at room temperature

½ cup confectioner's sugar

1 teaspoon pure vanilla extract

½ cup finely chopped toasted almonds (see How To Toast and Skin Nuts)

Filling

2 ounces semisweet or bittersweet chocolate, chopped

2 tablespoons unsalted butter

⅓ cup almonds, toasted and finely chopped

1. In a large bowl, sift together the flour, cocoa, and salt.

2. In a large bowl, with an electric mixer at medium speed, beat the butter and sugar until light and fluffy, about 2 minutes. Beat in the vanilla. Stir in the dry ingredients and the almonds until blended, about 1 minute more. Cover with plastic and chill in the refrigerator 1 hour up to overnight.

3. Preheat the oven to 350°F. Have ready 2 ungreased baking sheets. Roll teaspoonfuls of the dough into ¾-inch balls. Place the balls 1 inch apart on the baking sheets. With your fingers, press the balls to flatten them slightly. Bake the cookies until firm but not browned, 10 to 12 minutes. Have ready 2 large cooling racks.

4. Transfer the baking sheets to the racks. Let the cookies cool 5 minutes on the baking sheets, then transfer them to the racks to cool completely.

5. Bring about 2 inches of water to a simmer in the bottom half of a double boiler or a small saucepan. Place the chocolate and the butter in the top half of the double boiler or in a small heatproof bowl that fits comfortably over the saucepan. Place the bowl

over the simmering water. Let stand uncovered until the chocolate is softened. Stir until smooth. Stir in the almonds.

6. Spread a small amount of the filling mixture on the bottom of one cookie. Place a second cookie bottom-side down on the filling and press together lightly. Place the cookies on a wire rack until the filling is set. Repeat with the remaining cookies and filling. Store in an airtight container in the refrigerator up to 1 week.

No-Bake Chocolate "Salame"

Salame del Cioccolato

Makes 32 cookies

Crunchy chocolate nut slices that require no baking are a specialty of Piedmont. Other cookies can be substituted for the amaretti, if you prefer, such as vanilla or chocolate wafers, graham crackers, or shortbread. These are best made a few days ahead, to allow the flavors to blend. If you prefer not use the liqueur, substitute a spoonful of orange juice.

18 amaretti cookies

⅓ cup sugar

⅓ cup unsweetened cocoa powder

½ cup (1 stick) unsalted butter, softened

1 tablespoon grappa or rum

⅓ cup chopped walnuts

1. Place the cookies in a plastic bag. Crush the cookies with a rolling pin or heavy object. There should be about ¾ cup of crumbs.

2. Place the crumbs in a large bowl. With a wooden spoon, stir in the sugar and cocoa. Add the butter and grappa. Stir until the dry ingredients are moistened and blended. Stir in the walnuts.

3. Place a 14-inch sheet of plastic wrap on a flat surface. Pour the dough mixture onto the plastic wrap. Shape the dough into an 8 × 2 1/2–inch log. Roll the log in the plastic wrap, folding the ends over to enclose it completely. Refrigerate the log at least 24 hours and up to 3 days.

4. Cut the log into 1/4-inch-thick slices. Serve chilled. Store the cookies in an airtight plastic container in the refrigerator up to 2 weeks.

Prato Biscuits

Biscotti di Prato

Makes about 4½ dozen

In the town of Prato in Tuscany, these are the classic biscotti to dip in vin santo, the great dessert wine of the region. Eaten plain, they are rather dry, so do provide a beverage for dunking them.

2½ cups all-purpose flour

1½ teaspoons baking powder

1 teaspoon salt

4 large eggs

¾ cup sugar

1 teaspoon grated lemon zest

1 teaspoon grated orange zest

1 teaspoon pure vanilla extract

1 cup toasted almonds (see How To Toast and Skin Nuts)

1. Place a rack in the center of the oven. Preheat the oven to 325°F. Grease and flour a large baking sheet.

2. In a medium bowl, sift together the flour, baking powder, and salt.

3. In a large bowl with an electric mixer, beat the eggs and sugar on medium speed until light and foamy, about 3 minutes. Beat in the lemon and orange zests and vanilla. On low speed, stir in the dry ingredients, then stir in the almonds.

4. Lightly dampen your hands. Shape the dough into two 14 × 2-inch logs. Place the logs on the prepared baking sheet several inches apart. Bake for 30 minutes or until firm and golden.

5. Remove the baking sheet from the oven and reduce the oven heat to 300°F. Let the logs cool on the baking sheet for 20 minutes.

6. Slide the logs onto a cutting board. With a large heavy chef's knife, cut the logs on the diagonal into $1/2$-inch-thick slices. Lay the slices on the baking sheet. Bake 20 minutes or until lightly golden.

7. Transfer the cookies to wire racks to cool. Store in an airtight container.

Umbrian Fruit and Nut Biscotti

Tozzetti

Makes 80

Made without fat, these cookies keep a long time in an airtight container. The flavor actually improves, so plan to make them several days before serving them.

3 cups all-purpose flour

½ cup cornstarch

2 teaspoons baking powder

3 large eggs

3 egg yolks

2 tablespoons Marsala, vin santo, or sherry

1 cup sugar

1 cup raisins

1 cup almonds

¼ cup chopped candied orange peel

¼ cup chopped candied citron

1 teaspoon anise seeds

1. Preheat the oven to 350°F. Grease 2 large baking sheets.

2. In a medium bowl, sift together the flour, cornstarch, and baking powder.

3. In a large bowl with an electric mixer, beat together the eggs, yolks, and Marsala. Add the sugar and beat until well blended, about 3 minutes. Stir in the dry ingredients, the raisins, almonds, peel, citron and anise seeds until blended. The dough will be stiff. If necessary, turn the dough out onto a countertop and knead it until blended.

4. Divide the dough into quarters. Dampen your hands with cool water and shape each quarter into a 10-inch log. Place the logs 2 inches apart on the prepared baking sheets.

5. Bake the logs 20 minutes or until they feel firm when pressed in the center and are golden brown around the edges. Remove the logs from the oven but leave the oven on. Let the logs cool 5 minutes on the baking sheets.

6. Slide the logs onto a cutting board. With a large chef's knife, cut them into $1/2$-inch-thick slices. Place the slices on the baking sheets and bake 10 minutes or until lightly toasted.

7. Have ready 2 large cooling racks. Transfer the cookies to the racks. Let cool completely. Store in an airtight container up to 2 weeks.

Lemon Nut Biscotti

Biscotti al Limone

Makes 48

Lemon and almonds flavor these biscotti.

1½ cups all-purpose flour

1 teaspoon baking powder

¼ teaspoon salt

½ cup (1 stick) unsalted butter, at room temperature

½ cup sugar

2 large eggs, at room temperature

2 teaspoons freshly grated lemon zest

1 cup toasted almonds, coarsely chopped

1. Place a rack in the center of the oven. Preheat the oven to 350°F. Grease and flour a large baking sheet.

2. In a bowl, sift together the flour, baking powder, and salt.

3. In a large bowl with an electric mixer, beat the butter and sugar until light and fluffy, about 2 minutes. Beat in the eggs one at a time. Add the lemon zest, scraping the inside of the bowl with a rubber spatula. Gradually stir in the flour mixture and the nuts until blended.

4. Divide the dough in half. With moistened hands, shape each piece into a 12 × 2–inch log on the prepared baking sheet. Bake for 20 minutes or until the logs are lightly browned and firm when pressed in the center. Remove the pan from the oven, but do not turn off the heat. Let the logs cool 10 minutes on the baking sheet.

5. Slide the logs onto a cutting board. Cut the logs into $1/2$-inch-thick slices. Place the slices on the baking sheet. Bake for 10 minutes or until the cookies are lightly toasted.

6. Have ready 2 large cooling racks. Transfer the cookies to the racks. Let cool completely. Store in an airtight container up to 2 weeks.

Walnut Biscotti

Biscotti di Noce

Makes about 80

Olive oil can be used for baking in a wide range of recipes. Use a mild-flavored extra-virgin olive oil. It complements many types of nuts and citrus fruits. Here is a biscotti recipe I developed for an article in the Washington Post about baking with olive oil.

2 cups all-purpose flour

1 teaspoon baking powder

1 teaspoon salt

2 large eggs, at room temperature

2/3 cup sugar

1/2 cup extra-virgin olive oil

1/2 teaspoon grated lemon zest

2 cups toasted walnuts (see How To Toast and Skin Nuts)

1. Preheat the oven to 325°F. Grease 2 large baking sheets.

2. In a large bowl, combine the flour, baking powder, and salt.

3. In another large bowl, whisk the eggs, sugar, oil, and lemon zest until well blended. With a wooden spoon, stir in the dry ingredients just until blended. Stir in the walnuts.

4. Divide the dough into four pieces. Shape the pieces into 12 × $1^1/_2$–inch logs, placing them several inches apart on the prepared baking sheets. Bake for 20 to 25 minutes or until lightly browned. Remove from the oven, but do not turn it off. Let the cookies cool on the baking sheets 10 minutes.

5. Slide the logs onto a cutting board. With a large heavy knife, cut the logs diagonally into $^1/_2$-inch slices. Lay the slices on the baking sheets and return the sheets to the oven. Bake 10 minutes or until toasted and golden.

6. Have ready 2 large cooling racks. Transfer the cookies to the racks. Let cool completely. Store in an airtight container up to 2 weeks.

Almond Macaroons

Amaretti

Makes 3 dozen

In southern Italy, these are made by grinding up both sweet and bitter almonds. Bitter almonds, which come from a particular variety of almond tree, are not sold in the United States. They have a flavor component similar to cyanide, a lethal poison, so they are not approved for commercial use. The closest we can come to the correct flavor is commercial almond paste and a little almond extract. Do not confuse almond paste with marzipan, which is similar, but has a higher sugar content. Buy the almond paste sold in cans for best flavor. If you can't find it, ask at your local bakery to see if they will sell you some.

These cookies stick, so I bake them on nonstick baking mats known as Silpat. The mats never need greasing, are easy to clean, and reusable. You can find them at good kitchen supply stores. If you don't have the mats, the baking pans can be lined with parchment paper or aluminum foil.

1 (8-ounce) can almond paste, crumbled

1 cup sugar

2 large egg whites, at room temperature

¼ teaspoon almond extract

36 candied cherries or whole almonds

1. Preheat the oven to 350°F. Line 2 large baking sheets with parchment paper or aluminum foil.

2. Crumble the almond paste into a large bowl. With an electric mixer on low speed, beat in the sugar until blended. Add the egg whites and almond extract. Increase the speed to medium and beat until very smooth, about 3 minutes.

3. Scoop up 1 tablespoon of the batter and lightly roll it into a ball. Dampen your fingertips with cool water if necessary to prevent sticking. Place the balls about one inch apart on the prepared baking sheet. Press a cherry or almond into the top of the dough.

4. Bake 18 to 20 minutes or until the cookies are lightly browned. Let cool briefly on the baking sheet.

5. With a thin metal spatula, transfer the cookies to wire racks to cool completely. Store the cookies in airtight containers. (If you want to keep these cookies for more than a day or two, freeze

them to maintain their soft texture. They can be eaten directly from the freezer.)

Pine Nut Macaroons

Biscotti di Pinoli

Makes 40

I have made many variations of these cookies over the years. This version is my favorite because it is made with both almond paste and ground almonds for both flavor and texture and has the added rich flavor of toasted pine nuts (pignoli).

1 (8-ounce) can almond paste

⅓ cup finely ground blanched almonds

2 large egg whites

1 cup confectioner's sugar, plus more for decorating

2 cups pine nuts or slivered almonds

1. Place a rack in the center of the oven. Preheat the oven to 350°F. Grease a large baking sheet.

2. In a large bowl, crumble the almond paste. With an electric mixer on medium speed, beat in the almonds, egg whites, and 1 cup of confectioner's sugar until smooth.

3. Scoop up a tablespoon of the batter. Roll the batter in the pine nuts, covering it completely and forming a ball. Place the ball on the prepared baking sheet. Repeat with the remaining ingredients, placing the balls about 1 inch apart.

4. Bake 18 to 20 minutes or until lightly browned. Place the baking sheet on a cooling rack. Let the cookies cool 2 minutes on the baking sheet.

5. Transfer the cookies to racks to cool completely. Dust with confectioner's sugar. Store in an airtight container in the refrigerator up to 1 week.

Hazelnut Bars

Nocciolate

Makes 6 dozen

These tender, crumbly bars are packed with nuts. They barely hold together and melt in the mouth. Serve them with chocolate ice cream.

2 ⅓ cups all-purpose flour

1½ cups peeled, toasted hazelnuts, finely chopped (see How To Toast and Skin Nuts)

1½ cups sugar

½ teaspoon salt

1 cup (2 sticks) unsalted butter, melted and cooled

1 large egg plus 1 egg yolk, beaten

1. Place a rack in the center of the oven. Preheat the oven to 350°F. Grease a 15 × 10 × 1–inch jelly roll pan.

2. In a large bowl with a wooden spoon, stir together the flour, nuts, sugar, and salt. Add the butter and stir until evenly

moistened. Add the eggs. Stir until well blended and the mixture holds together.

3. Pour the mixture into the prepared pan. Firmly pat it out into an even layer.

4. Bake 30 minutes or until golden brown. While still hot, cut into 2 × 1-inch rectangles.

5. Let cool 10 minutes in the pan. Transfer the cookies to large racks to cool completely.

Walnut Butter Cookies

Biscotti di Noce

Makes 5 dozen

Nutty and buttery, these crescent-shaped cookies from Piedmont are perfect for Christmas. Though they are often made with hazelnuts, I like to use walnuts. Almonds can also be substituted.

These cookies can be made entirely in the food processor. If you don't have one, grind the nuts and sugar in a blender or nut grinder, then stir in the remaining ingredients by hand.

1 cup walnut pieces

⅓ cup sugar plus 1 cup more for rolling the cookies

2 cups all-purpose flour

1 cup (2 sticks) unsalted butter, at room temperature

1. Preheat oven to 350°F. Grease and flour 2 large baking sheets.

2. In a food processor, combine the walnuts and sugar. Process until the nuts are finely chopped. Add the flour and process until blended.

3. Add the butter a little at a time and pulse to blend. Remove the dough from the container and squeeze it together with your hands.

4. Pour the remaining 1 cup of sugar into a shallow bowl. Pinch off a piece of dough the size of a walnut and form it into a ball. Shape the ball into a crescent, tapering the ends. Gently roll the crescent in sugar. Place the crescent on a prepared baking sheet. Repeat with the remaining dough and sugar, placing each cookie about 1 inch apart.

5. Bake 15 minutes or until lightly browned. Place the baking sheets on wire racks to cool 5 minutes.

6. Transfer the cookies to the racks to cool completely. Store in an airtight container up to 2 weeks.

Rainbow Cookies

Biscotti Tricolori

Makes about 4 dozen

Though I have never seen them in Italy, these "rainbow," or tricolored, cookies with a chocolate glaze are a favorite at Italian and other bakeries in the United States. Unfortunately, they are often colored garishly and can be dry and tasteless.

Try this recipe and you will see how good these cookies can be. They are a bit fussy to make, but the results are very pretty and delicious. If you prefer not to use food coloring, the cookies will still be attractive. For convenience, it is best to have three identical baking pans. But you can still make the cookies with only one pan if you bake one batch of dough at a time. The finished cookies keep well in the refrigerator.

8 ounces almond paste

1½ cups (3 sticks) unsalted butter

1 cup sugar

4 large eggs, separated

¼ teaspoon salt

2 cups unbleached all-purpose flour

10 drops red food coloring, or to taste (optional)

10 drops green food coloring, or to taste (optional)

½ cup apricot preserves

½ cup seedless raspberry jam

1 (6-ounce) package semisweet chocolate chips

1. Preheat the oven to 350°F. Grease three 13 × 9 × 2– inch identical baking pans. Line the pans with wax paper and grease the paper.

2. Crumble the almond paste into a large mixer bowl. Add the butter, $1/2$ cup of the sugar, the egg yolks, and salt. Beat until light and fluffy. Stir in the flour just until blended.

3. In another large bowl, with clean beaters, beat the egg whites on medium speed until foamy. Gradually beat in the remaining sugar. Increase the speed to high. Continue beating until the egg whites form soft peaks when the beaters are lifted.

4. With a rubber spatula, fold $1/3$ of the whites into the yolk mixture to lighten it. Gradually fold in the remaining whites.

5. Scoop $1/3$ of the batter into one bowl, and another $1/3$ into another bowl. If using the food coloring, fold the red into one bowl and the green into the other.

6. Spread each bowl of batter into a separate prepared pan, smoothing it out evenly with a spatula. Bake the layers 10 to 12 minutes, until the cake is just set and very lightly colored around the edges. Let cool in the pan for 5 minutes, then lift the layers onto cooling racks, leaving the wax paper attached. Let cool completely.

7. Using the paper to lift one layer, invert the cake and place it paper-side up on a large tray. Carefully peel off the paper. Spread with a thin layer of the raspberry jam.

8. Set a second layer paper-side up on top of the first. Remove the paper and spread the cake with the apricot jam.

9. Place the remaining layer paper-side up on top. Peel off the paper. With a large heavy knife and a ruler as a guide, trim the edges of the cake to make the layers straight and even all around.

10. Bring about 2 inches of water to a simmer in the bottom half of a double boiler or a small saucepan. Place the chocolate chips in the top half of the double boiler or in a small heatproof bowl that fits comfortably over the saucepan. Place the bowl over the simmering water. Let stand uncovered until the chocolate is softened. Stir until smooth. Pour the melted chocolate on top of the cake layers and spread it smooth with a spatula. Refrigerate until the chocolate is just beginning to set, about 30 minutes. (Don't let it get too hard, or it will crack when you cut it.)

11. Remove the cake from the refrigerator. Using a ruler or other straight edge as a guide, cut the cake lengthwise into 6 strips by first cutting it into thirds, then cutting each third in half. Cut crosswise into 5 strips. Chill the cut cake in the pan in the refrigerator until the chocolate is firm. Serve or transfer the cookies to an airtight container and store in the refrigerator. These keep well for several weeks.

Christmas Fig Cookies

Cuccidati

Makes 18 large cookies

I can't imagine Christmas without these cookies. For many Sicilians, making them is a family project. The women mix and roll the dough, while the men chop and grind the filling ingredients. The children decorate the filled cookies. They are traditionally cut into many fanciful shapes resembling birds, leaves, or flowers. Some families make dozens of them to give away to friends and neighbors.

Dough

2½ cups all-purpose flour

⅓ cup sugar

2 teaspoons baking powder

½ teaspoon salt

6 tablespoons unsalted butter

2 large eggs, at room temperature

1 teaspoon pure vanilla extract

Filling

2 cups moist dried figs, stems removed

½ cup raisins

1 cup walnuts, toasted and chopped

½ cup chopped semisweet chocolate (about 2 ounces)

⅓ cup honey

¼ cup orange juice

1 teaspoon orange zest

1 teaspoon ground cinnamon

⅛ teaspoon ground cloves

Assembly

1 egg yolk beaten with 1 teaspoon water

Colored candy sprinkles

1. Prepare the dough: In a large bowl, combine the flour, sugar, baking powder, and salt. Cut in the butter, using an electric

mixer or pastry blender, until the mixture resembles coarse crumbs.

2. In a bowl, whisk the eggs and vanilla. Add the eggs to the dry ingredients, stirring with a wooden spoon until the dough is evenly moistened. If the dough is too dry, blend in a little cold water a few drops at a time.

3. Gather the dough into a ball and place it on a sheet of plastic wrap. Flatten it into a disk and wrap well. Refrigerate at least 1 hour or overnight.

4. Prepare the filling: In a food processor or meat grinder, grind the figs, raisins, and nuts until coarsely chopped. Stir in the remaining ingredients. Cover and refrigerate if not using within the hour.

5. To assemble the pastries, preheat the oven to 375°F. Grease two large baking sheets.

6. Cut the dough into 6 pieces. On a lightly floured surface, roll each piece into a log about 4 inches long.

7. With a floured rolling pin, roll one log into a 9 × 5-inch rectangle. Trim the edges.

8. Spoon a ¾-inch strip of the filling lengthwise slightly to one side of the center of the rolled out dough. Fold one long side of the dough over to the other and press the edges together to seal. Cut the filled dough crosswise into 3 even pieces.

9. With a sharp knife, cut slits ¾-inch long at ½-inch intervals through the filling and dough. Curving them slightly to open the slits and reveal the fig filling, place the pastries one inch apart on the baking sheets.

10. Brush the pastry with the egg wash. Drizzle with candy sprinkles if desired. Repeat with the remaining ingredients.

11. Bake the cookies 20 to 25 minutes or until golden brown.

12. Cool the cookies on wire racks. Store in an airtight container in the refrigerator up to 1 month.

Almond Brittle

Croccante or Torrone

Makes 10 to 12 servings

Sicilians make these sweets with pine nuts, pistachios, or sesame seeds in place of the almonds. A lemon is perfect to smooth out the hot syrup.

Vegetable oil

2 cups sugar

¼ cup honey

2 cups almonds (10 ounces)

1 whole lemon, washed and dried

1. Brush a marble surface or a metal baking sheet with neutral-flavored vegetable oil.

2. In a medium saucepan, combine the sugar and honey. Cook over medium-low heat, stirring occasionally, until the sugar begins to melt, about 20 minutes. Bring to a simmer and cook without stirring 5 minutes more or until the syrup is clear.

3. Add the nuts and cook until the syrup is amber-colored, about 3 minutes. Carefully pour the hot syrup onto the prepared surface, using the lemon to smooth the nuts to a single layer. Let cool completely. When the brittle is cool and hard, after about 30 minutes, slide a thin metal spatula underneath it. Lift the brittle and break it into $1^{1}/_{2}$-inch pieces. Store in airtight containers at room temperature.

Sicilian Nut Rolls

Mostaccioli

Makes 64 cookies

At one time these cookies were made with mosto cotto, concentrated wine grape juice. Today's cooks use honey.

Dough

3 cups all-purpose flour

½ cup sugar

1 teaspoon salt

½ cup shortening

4 tablespoons (½ stick) unsalted butter, at room temperature

2 large eggs

2 to 3 tablespoons cold milk

Filling

1 cup toasted almonds

1 cup toasted walnuts

½ cup toasted and skinned hazelnuts

¼ cup sugar

¼ cup honey

2 teaspoons orange zest

¼ teaspoon ground cinnamon

Confectioner's sugar

1. In a large bowl, combine the flour, sugar, and salt. Cut in the shortening and butter until the mixture resembles coarse crumbs.

2. In a small bowl, whisk the eggs with two tablespoons of the milk. Add the mixture to the dry ingredients, stirring until the dough is evenly moistened. If needed, blend in a little more milk.

3. Gather the dough into a ball and place it on a sheet of plastic wrap. Flatten it into a disk and wrap well. Refrigerate 1 hour up to overnight.

4. Process the nuts and sugar in a food processor. Process until fine. Add the honey, zest, and cinnamon, and process until

blended. Preheat the oven to 350°F. Grease 2 large baking sheets.

5. Divide the dough into 4 pieces. Roll out one piece between two sheets of plastic wrap to form a square slightly larger than 8 inches. Trim the edges and cut the dough into 2-inch squares. Place a heaping teaspoon of the filling along one side of each square. Roll up the dough to enclose the filling completely. Place seam-side down on the baking pan. Repeat with the remaining dough and filling, placing the cookies 1 inch apart.

6. Bake 18 minutes or until the cookies are lightly browned. Transfer the cookies to wire racks to cool. Store in a tightly sealed container up to 2 weeks. Sprinkle with confectioner's sugar before serving.

Sponge Cake

Pan di Spagna

Makes two 8- or 9-inch layers

This classic and versatile Italian sponge cake works well with fillings such as fruit preserves, whipped cream, pastry cream, ice cream, or ricotta cream. The cake also freezes well, so it is convenient to have on hand for quick desserts.

Butter for the pan

6 large eggs, at room temperature

⅔ cup sugar

1½ teaspoons pure vanilla extract

1 cup sifted all-purpose flour

1. Place the rack in the center of the oven. Preheat the oven to 375°F. Butter two 8- or 9-inch layer cake pans. Line the bottom of the pans with circles of waxed paper or parchment paper. Butter the paper. Dust the pans with flour and tap out the excess.

2. In a large bowl with an electric mixer, begin beating the eggs on low speed. Slowly add the sugar, gradually increasing the mixer speed to high. Add the vanilla. Beat the eggs until thick and pale yellow, about 7 minutes.

3. Place the flour in a fine-mesh strainer. Shake about one-third of the flour over the egg mixture. Gradually and very gently fold in the flour with a rubber spatula. Repeat, adding the flour in 2 additions and folding it in until there are no streaks.

4. Spread the batter evenly in the prepared pans. Bake 20 to 25 minutes or until the cakes spring back when pressed lightly in the center and the top is lightly browned. Have ready 2 cooling racks. Cool the cakes 10 minutes in the pans on the wire racks.

5. Invert the cakes onto the racks and remove the pans. Carefully peel off the paper. Let cool completely. Serve immediately or cover with an inverted bowl and store at room temperature up to 2 days.

Citrus Sponge Cake

Torta di Agrumi

Serves 10 to 12

Olive oil gives this cake a distinctive flavor and texture. Use a mild olive oil or the flavor could be intrusive. Because it does not contain butter, milk, or other dairy products, this cake is good for people who cannot eat those foods.

This is a big cake, though it is very light and airy. To bake it, you will need a 10-inch tube pan with a removable bottom—the kind used for angel cakes.

A little bit of cream of tartar, available in the spice section of most supermarkets, helps to stabilize the egg whites in this large cake.

2¼ cups plain cake flour (not self-rising)

1 tablespoon baking powder

1 teaspoon salt

6 large eggs, separated, at room temperature

1¼ cups sugar

1½ teaspoons orange zest

1½ teaspoons grated lemon zest

¾ cup freshly squeezed orange juice

½ cup extra-virgin olive oil

1 teaspoon pure vanilla extract

¼ teaspoon cream of tartar

1. Place the oven rack in the lower third of the oven. Preheat the oven to 325°F. In a large bowl, sift together the flour, baking powder, and salt.

2. In a large bowl with an electric mixer, beat the egg yolks, 1 cup of the sugar, the orange and lemon zests, the orange juice, oil, and vanilla extract until smooth, about 5 minutes. With a rubber spatula, fold the liquid into the dry ingredients.

3. In another large bowl with clean beaters, beat the egg whites on medium speed until foamy. Gradually add the remaining ¼ cup of sugar and the cream of tartar. Increase the speed to high. Beat until soft peaks form when the beaters are lifted, about 5 minutes. Fold the whites into the batter.

4. Scrape the batter into an ungreased 10-inch tube pan with a removable bottom. Bake 55 minutes or until the cake is golden brown and a toothpick inserted in the center comes out clean.

5. Place the pan upside down on a cooling rack and let the cake cool completely. Run a thin-blade knife around the inside of the pan to loosen the cake. Lift out the cake and the bottom of the pan. Slide the knife under the cake and remove the pan bottom. Serve immediately, or cover with an overturned bowl and store at room temperature up to 2 days.

Lemon Olive-Oil Cake

Torta di Limone

Makes 8 servings

A light, lemony cake from Puglia that is always a pleasure to have on hand.

1½ cups plain cake flour (not self-rising)

1½ teaspoons baking powder

½ teaspoon salt

3 large eggs, at room temperature

1 cup sugar

⅓ cup olive oil

1 teaspoon pure vanilla extract

1 teaspoon grated lemon zest

¼ cup freshly squeezed lemon juice

1. Place the rack in the lowest third of the oven. Preheat oven to 350°F. Grease a 9-inch springform pan.

2. In a large bowl, sift together the flour, baking powder, and salt.

3. Break the eggs into a large electric mixer bowl. Beat on medium speed until thick and pale yellow, about 5 minutes. Slowly add in the sugar and beat 3 minutes more. Slowly add the oil. Beat one minute more. Add the vanilla and lemon zest.

4. With a rubber spatula, fold in the dry ingredients in three additions, alternating with the lemon juice in two additions.

5. Scrape the batter into the prepared pan. Bake 35 to 40 minutes or until the cake is golden brown and springs back when pressed in the center.

6. Turn the pan upside down on a wire rack. Let cool completely. Run a knife around the outside rim and remove it. Serve immediately, or cover with an overturned bowl and store at room temperature up to 2 days.

Marble Cake

Torta Marmorata

Makes 8 to 10 servings

Breakfast is not given a lot of attention in Italy. Eggs and cereal are rarely eaten, and most Italians get by on coffee with toast or perhaps a plain cookie or two. Hotel breakfasts often overcompensate for foreign tastes with a lavish variety of cold meats, cheeses, fruit, eggs, yogurt, bread, and pastries. At one hotel in Venice, I spotted a magnificent marble cake, one of my personal favorite cakes, proudly displayed on a cake stand. It was heavenly with a cup of cappuccino, and I would have enjoyed it equally at teatime. The waiter told me the cake was delivered fresh daily from a local bakery where it was a specialty. This is my version, inspired by the one in Venice.

1⅓ cups plain cake flour (not self-rising)

1½ teaspoons baking powder

½ teaspoon salt

3 large eggs, at room temperature

1 cup sugar

⅓ cup vegetable oil

1 teaspoon pure vanilla extract

¼ teaspoon almond extract

½ cup milk

2 ounces bittersweet or semisweet chocolate, melted and cooled

1. Place the oven rack in the lowest third of the oven. Preheat the oven to 325°F. Grease and flour a 10-inch tube pan and tap out the excess flour.

2. In a large bowl, sift together the flour, baking powder, and salt.

3. In another large bowl, with an electric mixer, beat the eggs on medium speed until thick and pale yellow, about 5 minutes. Slowly beat in the sugar a tablespoon at a time. Continue beating 2 minutes more.

4. Gradually beat in the oil and extracts. Fold in the flour in 3 additions, alternately adding the milk in two additions.

5. Remove about 1½ cups of the batter and place it in a small bowl. Set aside. Scrape the remaining batter into the prepared pan.

6. Fold the melted chocolate into the reserved batter. Place large spoonfuls of the chocolate batter on top of the batter in the pan. To swirl the batter, hold a table knife with the tip down. Insert the knife blade down through batter, running it gently all around the pan at least 2 times.

7. Bake 40 minutes or until the cake is golden brown and a toothpick comes out clean when inserted in the center. Let cool on a rack 10 minutes.

8. Invert the cake onto the rack and remove the pan. Turn the cake right-side up on another rack. Let cool completely. Serve immediately, or cover with an inverted bowl and store at room temperature up to 2 days.

Rum Cake

Baba au Rhum

Makes 8 to 10 servings

According to a popular story, this cake was invented by a Polish king who found his babka, a Polish yeast cake, too dry and poured a glass of rum on it. His creation was named baba, after Ali Baba of the Arabian Nights. How it became popular in Naples is not certain, but it has been for some time.

Because it is leavened with yeast rather than baking powder, baba has a spongy texture, perfect for absorbing the rum syrup. Some versions are baked in miniature muffin pans, while others have a pastry cream filling. I like to serve this with strawberries and whipped cream on the side—not typical, but delicious, and makes a lovely presentation.

1 package (2½ teaspoons) active dry yeast or instant yeast

¼ cup warm milk (100° to 110°F)

6 large eggs

2⅔ cups all-purpose flour

3 tablespoons sugar

½ teaspoon salt

¾ cup (1½ sticks) unsalted butter, at room temperature

Syrup

2 cups sugar

2 cups water

2 (2-inch) strips lemon zest

¼ cup rum

1. Grease a 10-inch tube pan.

2. Sprinkle the yeast over the warm milk. Let stand until creamy, about 1 minute, then stir until dissolved.

3. In a large mixing bowl, with an electric mixer on medium speed, beat the eggs until foamy, about 1 minute. Beat in the flour, sugar, and salt. Add the yeast and butter and beat until well blended, about 2 minutes

4. Scrape the dough into the prepared pan. Cover with plastic wrap and let stand in a warm place 1 hour or until the dough has doubled in volume.

5. Place a rack in the center of the oven. Preheat the oven to 400°F. Bake the cake 30 minutes or until it is golden and a toothpick inserted in the center comes out clean.

6. Invert the cake onto a cooling rack. Remove the pan and let cool for 10 minutes.

7. To make the syrup, combine the sugar, water, and lemon zest in a medium saucepan. Bring the mixture to a boil and stir until the sugar is dissolved, about 2 minutes. Remove the lemon zest. Stir in the rum. Set aside $1/4$ cup of the syrup.

8. Return the cake to the pan. With a fork, poke holes all over the surface. Slowly spoon the syrup over the cake while both are still hot. Let cool completely in the pan.

9. Just before serving, invert the cake onto a serving plate Drizzle with the remaining syrup. Serve immediately. Store covered with an overturned bowl at room temperature up to 2 days.

Grandmother's Cake

Torta della Nonna

Makes 8 servings

I couldn't decide whether to include this recipe—called torta della nonna—with the tarts or with the cakes; however, because Tuscans call it a torta, I include it with the cakes. It consists of two layers of pastry filled with a thick pastry cream. I don't know whose grandmother invented it, but everyone loves her cake. There are many variations, some including lemon flavoring.

1 cup milk

3 large egg yolks

⅓ cup sugar

1½ teaspoons pure vanilla extract

2 tablespoons all-purpose flour

2 tablespoons orange liqueur or rum

Dough

1⅔ cup all-purpose flour

½ cup sugar

1 teaspoon baking powder

½ teaspoon salt

½ cup (1 stick) unsalted butter, at room temperature

1 large egg, lightly beaten

1 teaspoon pure vanilla extract

1 egg yolk beaten with 1 teaspoon water, for egg wash

2 tablespoons pine nuts

Confectioner's sugar

1. In a medium saucepan, heat the milk over low heat until bubbles form around the edges. Remove from the heat.

2. In a medium bowl, whisk the egg yolks, sugar, and vanilla until pale yellow, about 5 minutes. Whisk in the flour. Gradually add the hot milk, whisking constantly. Transfer the mixture to the saucepan and cook over medium heat, stirring constantly, until boiling. Reduce the heat and simmer for 1 minute. Scrape the mixture into a bowl. Stir in the liqueur. Place a piece of plastic wrap directly on the surface of the custard to prevent a skin from forming. Refrigerate 1 hour up to overnight.

3. Place the rack in the center of the oven. Preheat the oven to 350°F. Grease a 9 × 2–inch round cake pan.

4. Prepare the dough: In a large bowl, stir together the flour, sugar, baking powder, and salt. With a pastry blender, cut in the butter until the mixture resembles coarse crumbs. Add the egg and vanilla and stir until a dough forms. Divide the dough in half.

5. Scatter half of the dough evenly in the bottom of the prepared pan. Press the dough into the bottom of the pan and $1/2$ inch up the sides. Spread the chilled custard over the center of the dough, leaving a 1-inch border around the edge.

6. On a lightly floured surface, roll out the remaining dough to a $9^1/_2$-inch circle. Place the dough over the filling. Press the edges of the dough together to seal. Brush the egg wash over the top of the cake. Sprinkle with the pine nuts. With a small knife, make several slits in the top to allow steam to escape.

7. Bake 35 to 40 minutes, or until golden brown on top. Let cool in the pan on a rack for 10 minutes.

8. Invert the cake onto the rack, then invert onto another rack to cool completely. Sprinkle with confectioner's sugar before serving. Serve immediately, or wrap the cake in plastic wrap and refrigerate up to 8 hours. Wrap and store in the refrigerator.

Apricot Almond Cake

Torta di Albicocche e Mandorle

Makes 8 servings

Apricots and almonds are very compatible flavors. If you can't find fresh apricots, substitute peaches or nectarines.

Topping

⅔ cup sugar

¼ cup water

12 to 14 apricots or 6 to 8 peaches, halved, pitted, and cut into ¼-inch-thick slices

Cake

1 cup all-purpose flour

1 teaspoon baking powder

½ teaspoon salt

½ cup almond paste

2 tablespoons unsalted butter

⅔ cup sugar

½ teaspoon pure vanilla extract

2 large eggs

⅔ cup milk

1. Prepare the topping: Place the sugar and water in a small heavy saucepan. Cook over medium heat, stirring occasionally, until the sugar is completely dissolved, about 3 minutes. When the mixture begins to boil, stop stirring and cook until the syrup starts to brown around the edges. Then gently swirl the pan over the heat until the syrup is an even golden brown, about 2 minutes more.

2. Protecting your hand with a pot holder, immediately pour the caramel into a 9 × 2-inch round cake pan. Tilt the pan to coat the bottom evenly. Let the caramel cool until set, about 5 minutes.

3. Place the oven rack in the center of the oven. Preheat the oven to 350°F. Arrange the sliced fruit, overlapping them slightly, in circles on top of the caramel.

4. Combine the flour, baking powder, and salt in a fine-mesh strainer set over a piece of wax paper. Sift the dry ingredients onto the paper.

5. In a large electric mixer bowl, beat the almond paste, butter, sugar, and vanilla until fluffy, about 4 minutes. Beat in the eggs one at a time, scraping the side of the bowl. Continue beating until smooth and well blended, about 4 minutes more.

6. With the mixer on low speed, stir in $1/3$ of the flour mixture. Add $1/3$ of the milk. Add the remaining flour mixture and milk in two more additions in the same way, ending with the flour. Stir just until smooth.

7. Pour the batter over the fruit. Bake 40 to 45 minutes or until the cake is golden and a toothpick inserted in the center comes out clean.

8. Let the cake cool in the pan on a wire rack 10 minutes. Run a thin metal spatula around the inside of the pan. Invert the cake onto a serving plate (the fruit will be on top) and let cool completely before serving. Serve immediately, or cover with an inverted bowl and store at room temperature up to 24 hours.

Summer Fruit Torte

Torta dell'Estate

Makes 8 servings

Soft stone fruits such as plums, apricots, peaches, and nectarines are ideal for this torte. Try making it with a combination of fruits.

12 to 16 prune plums or apricots, or 6 medium peaches or nectarines, halved, pitted, and cut into ½-inch slices

1 cup all-purpose flour

1 teaspoon baking powder

½ teaspoon salt

½ cup (1 stick) unsalted butter, at room temperature

⅔ cup plus 2 tablespoons sugar

1 large egg

1 teaspoon grated lemon zest

1 teaspoon pure vanilla extract

Confectioner's sugar

1. Place the rack in the center of the oven. Preheat the oven to 350°F. Grease a 9-inch springform pan.

2. In a large bowl, mix together the flour, baking powder, and salt.

3. In another large bowl, beat the butter with $2/3$ cup of the sugar until light and fluffy, about 3 minutes. Beat in the egg, lemon zest, and vanilla until smooth. Add the dry ingredients and stir just until blended, about 1 minute more.

4. Scrape the batter into the prepared pan. Arrange the fruit, overlapping it slightly, on top in concentric circles. Sprinkle with the remaining 2 tablespoons of sugar.

5. Bake 45 to 50 minutes or until the cake is golden brown and a toothpick inserted in the center comes out clean.

6. Let the cake cool in the pan on a wire rack 10 minutes, then remove the rim of the pan. Let the cake cool completely. Sprinkle with confectioner's sugar before serving. Serve immediately, or cover with an overturned bowl and store at room temperature up to 24 hours.

Autumn Fruit Torte

Torta del Autunno

Makes 8 servings

Apples, pears, figs, or plums are good in this simple cake. The batter forms a top layer that does not quite cover the fruit, allowing it to peek through the surface of the cake. I like to serve it slightly warm.

1½ cups all-purpose flour

1 teaspoon baking powder

½ teaspoon salt

2 large eggs

1 cup sugar

1 teaspoon pure vanilla extract

4 tablespoons unsalted butter, melted and cooled

2 medium apples or pears, peeled, cored, and sliced into thin wedges

Confectioner's sugar

1. Place the rack in the center of the oven. Preheat the oven to 350°F. Grease and flour a 9-inch springform cake pan. Tap out the excess flour.

2. In a bowl, stir together the flour, baking powder, and salt.

3. In a large bowl, beat the eggs with the sugar and vanilla until blended, about 2 minutes. Beat in the butter. Stir in the flour mixture until just blended, about 1 minute more.

4. Spread half of the batter in the prepared pan. Cover with the fruits. Drop the remaining batter on top by spoonfuls. Spread the batter evenly over the fruits. The layer will be thin. Don't be concerned if the fruit is not completely covered.

5. Bake 30 to 35 minutes or until the cake is golden brown and a toothpick inserted in the center comes out clean.

6. Let the cake cool 10 minutes in the pan on a wire rack. Remove the rim of the pan. Cool the cake completely on the rack. Serve warm or at room temperature with a sprinkle of confectioner's sugar. Store covered with a large inverted bowl at room temperature up to 24 hours.

Polenta and Pear Cake

Dolce di Polenta

Makes 8 servings

Yellow cornmeal adds a pleasant texture and warm golden color to this rustic cake from the Veneto.

1 cup all-purpose flour

⅓ cup finely ground yellow cornmeal

1 teaspoon baking powder

½ teaspoon salt

¾ cup (1½ sticks) unsalted butter, softened

¾ cup plus 2 tablespoons sugar

1 teaspoon pure vanilla extract

½ teaspoon grated lemon zest

2 large eggs

⅓ cup milk

1 large ripe pear, cored and thinly sliced

1. Place a rack in the center of the oven. Preheat the oven to 350°F. Grease and flour a 9-inch springform pan. Tap out the excess flour.

2. In a large bowl, sift together the flour, cornmeal, baking powder, and salt.

3. In a large bowl with an electric mixer, beat the butter, gradually adding $3/4$ cup of the sugar until light and fluffy, about 3 minutes. Beat in the vanilla and lemon zest. Beat in the eggs one at time, scraping the sides of the bowl. On low speed, stir in half of the dry ingredients. Add the milk. Stir in the remaining dry ingredients just until smooth, about 1 minute.

4. Spread the batter in the prepared pan. Arrange the pear slices on top, overlapping them slightly. Sprinkle the pear with the remaining 2 tablespoons of sugar.

5. Bake 45 minutes or until the cake is golden brown and a toothpick inserted in the center comes out clean.

6. Cool the cake in the pan 10 minutes on a wire rack. Remove the pan rim and cool the cake completely on the rack. Serve

immediately, or cover with a large inverted bowl and store at room temperature up to 24 hours.

Ricotta Cheesecake

Torta di Ricotta

Makes 12 servings

I like to think of this as an American-style Italian cheesecake. It is a large cake, though the flavor is delicate, with lemon zest and cinnamon. This cake is baked in a water bath so that it cooks evenly. The base of the pan is wrapped in foil to prevent the water from seeping into the pan.

1¼ cups sugar

⅓ cup all-purpose flour

½ teaspoon ground cinnamon

3 pounds whole or part-skim ricotta

8 large eggs

2 teaspoons pure vanilla extract

2 teaspoons grated lemon zest

1. Place a rack in the center of the oven. Preheat the oven to 350°F. Grease and flour a 9-inch springform pan. Tap out the excess

flour. Place the pan on a 12-inch square of heavy-duty aluminum foil. Mold the foil tightly around the base and about 2 inches up the sides of the pan so that water cannot seep in.

2. In a medium bowl, stir together the sugar, flour, and cinnamon.

3. In a large mixing bowl, whisk the ricotta until smooth. Beat in the eggs, vanilla, and lemon zest until well blended. (For a smoother texture, beat the ingredients with an electric mixer or process them in a food processor.) Whisk in the dry ingredients just until blended.

4. Pour the batter into the prepared pan. Set the pan in a large roasting pan and place it in the oven. Carefully pour hot water to a depth of 1 inch in the roasting pan. Bake $1^1/_2$ hours or until the top of the cake is golden and a toothpick inserted 2 inches from the center comes out clean.

5. Turn off the oven and prop the door open slightly. Let the cake cool in the turned off oven 30 minutes. Remove the cake from the oven and remove the foil wrapping. Cool to room temperature in the pan on a wire rack.

6. Serve at room temperature or refrigerate and serve slightly chilled. Store covered with an inverted bowl in the refrigerator up to 3 days.

Sicilian Ricotta Cake

Cassata

Makes 10 to 12 servings

Cassata is the glory of Sicilian desserts. It consists of two layers of pan di Spagna (Sponge Cake) filled with sweetened, flavored ricotta. The whole cake is frosted with two icings, one of tinted almond paste and the other flavored with lemon. Sicilians decorate the cake with glistening candied fruits and almond paste cutouts so that it looks like something out of a fairy tale.

Originally served only at Easter time, cassata is now found at celebrations throughout the year.

2 Sponge Cake layers

1 pound whole or part-skim ricotta

½ cup confectioner's sugar

1 teaspoon pure vanilla extract

¼ teaspoon ground cinnamon

½ cup chopped semisweet chocolate

2 tablespoons chopped candied orange peel

Icing

4 ounces almond paste

2 or 3 drops green food coloring

2 egg whites

¼ teaspoon grated lemon zest

1 tablespoon fresh lemon juice

2 cups confectioner's sugar

Candied or dried fruits, such as cherries, pineapple, or citron

1. Prepare the sponge cake, if necessary. Then, in a large bowl with a wire whisk, beat the ricotta, sugar, vanilla, and cinnamon until smooth and creamy. Fold in the chocolate and orange peel.

2. Place one cake layer on a serving plate. Spread the ricotta mixture on top. Place the second cake layer over the filling.

3. For the decoration, crumble the almond paste into a food processor fitted with the steel blade. Add one drop of the food coloring. Process until evenly tinted a light green, adding more

color if needed. Remove the almond paste and shape it into a short thick log.

4. Cut the almond paste into 4 lengthwise slices. Place one slice between two sheets of wax paper. With a rolling pin, flatten it into a narrow ribbon 3 inches long and $1/8$-inch thick. Unwrap and trim off any rough edges, reserving the scraps. Repeat with the remaining almond paste. The ribbons should be about the same width as the height of the cake. Wrap the almond paste ribbons end to end all around the sides of the cake, overlapping the ends slightly.

5. Gather the scraps of almond paste and reroll them. Cut into decorative shapes, such as stars, flowers, or leaves, with cookie cutters.

6. Prepare the icing: Whisk the egg whites, lemon zest, and juice. Add the confectioner's sugar and stir until smooth.

7. Spread the icing evenly over the top of the cake. Decorate the cake with the almond paste cutouts and the candied fruits. Cover with a large overturned bowl and refrigerate until serving time, up to 8 hours. Store leftovers covered in the refrigerator up to 2 days.

Ricotta Crumb Cake

Sbriciolata di Ricotta

Makes 8 servings

Brunch, a very American meal, is fashionable right now in Milan and other cities in northern Italy. This is my version of the ricotta-filled crumb cake I ate at brunch at a caffè not far from the Piazza del Duomo in the heart of Milan.

2½ cups all-purpose flour

½ teaspoon salt

½ teaspoon ground cinnamon

¾ cup (1½ sticks) unsalted butter

⅔ cup sugar

1 large egg

Filling

1 pound whole or part-skim ricotta

¼ cup sugar

1 teaspoon grated lemon zest

1 large egg, beaten

¼ cup raisins

Confectioner's sugar

1. Place a rack in the center of the oven. Preheat the oven to 350°F. Grease and flour a 9-inch springform pan. Tap out the excess flour.

2. In a large bowl, stir together the flour, salt, and cinnamon.

3. In a large bowl, with an electric mixer at medium speed, beat together the butter and sugar until light and fluffy, about 3 minutes. Beat in the egg. On low speed, stir in the dry ingredients until the mixture is blended and forms a firm dough, about 1 minute more.

4. Prepare the filling: Stir together the ricotta, sugar, and lemon zest until blended. Add the egg and stir well. Stir in the raisins.

5. Crumble 2/3 of the dough into the prepared pan. Pat the crumbs firmly to form the bottom crust. Spread with the ricotta mixture, leaving a 1/2-inch border all around. Crumble the remaining dough over the top, scattering the crumbs evenly.

6. Bake 40 to 45 minutes or until the cake is golden brown and a toothpick inserted in the center comes out clean. Let cool in the pan on a rack 10 minutes.

7. Run a thin metal spatula around the inside of the pan. Remove the pan rim and cool the cake completely. Sprinkle with confectioner's sugar before serving. Store covered with a large inverted bowl in the refrigerator up to 2 days.

Easter Wheat-Berry Cake

La Pastiera

Wheat berries add a slightly chewy texture to this traditional Neapolitan Easter cake. This was my father's mother's recipe, which she brought with her from Procida, an island off the coast of Naples. Neapolitans love this dessert, and you will find it in bakeries and restaurants in the area all year round. Both the crust and the filling are flavored with cinnamon and orange-flower water, a delicate essence made from orange blossoms that is frequently used in southern Italian desserts. It can be found in many gourmet stores, spice shops, and ethnic markets. Substitute fresh orange juice if you cannot find it. Hulled wheat is often found in Italian markets and natural food stores, or try the mail order sources.

Dough

3 cups all-purpose flour

½ teaspoon ground cinnamon

½ teaspoon salt

¾ cup (1½ sticks) unsalted butter, softened

1 cup confectioner's sugar

1 large egg

2 large egg yolks

2 teaspoons orange-flower water

Filling

4 ounces hulled wheat (about ½ cup)

½ teaspoon salt

½ cup (1 stick) unsalted butter, softened

1 teaspoon grated orange zest

1 pound (2 cups) whole or part-skim ricotta

4 large eggs, at room temperature

⅔ cup sugar

3 tablespoons orange-flower water

1 teaspoon ground cinnamon

½ cup very finely chopped candied citron

½ cup very finely chopped candied orange peel

Confectioner's sugar

1. Prepare the dough: In a large bowl, stir together the flour, cinnamon, and salt.

2. In a large bowl with an electric mixer on medium speed, beat the butter and confectioner's sugar until light and fluffy, about 3 minutes. Add the egg and yolks and beat until smooth. Beat in the orange-flower water. Add the dry ingredients and stir just until blended, about 1 minute more.

3. Shape 1/4 of the dough into a disk. Make a second disk with the remaining dough. Wrap each piece in plastic wrap and chill 1 hour up to overnight.

4. Prepare the filling: Place the wheat in a large bowl, add cold water to cover, and let soak overnight in the refrigerator. Drain the wheat.

5. Place the soaked wheat in a medium saucepan with cold water to cover. Add the salt and bring to a simmer over medium heat. Cook, stirring occasionally, until the wheat is tender, 20 to 30 minutes. Drain, and place in a large bowl. Stir in the butter and orange zest. Let cool.

6. Place the rack in the lower third of the oven. Preheat the oven to 350°F. Grease and flour a 9 × 3– inch springform pan. In a large bowl, whisk together the ricotta, eggs, sugar, orange-flower water, and cinnamon. Beat until blended. Stir in the wheat mixture, citron, and candied orange peel.

7. Roll out the larger piece of dough to a 16-inch circle. Drape the dough over the rolling pin. Using the pin to lift it, fit the dough into the pan, flattening out any wrinkles against the inside of the pan. Scrape the filling onto the dough and smooth the top.

8. Roll out the smaller piece of dough to a 10-inch circle. With a fluted pastry cutter, cut the dough into $1/2$-inch-wide strips. Lay the strips across the filling in a lattice pattern. Press the ends of the strips against the dough on the sides of the pan. Trim the dough, leaving $1/2$ inch of excess all around the rim, and fold the edge of the crust over the ends of the lattice strips. Press firmly to seal.

9. Bake 1 hour 10 minutes or until the cake is golden brown on top and a toothpick inserted in the center comes out clean.

10. Let the cake cool in the pan on a rack 15 minutes. Remove the rim of the pan and let the cake cool completely on a wire rack.

Just before serving, sprinkle with confectioner's sugar. Store covered with an inverted bowl in the refrigerator up to 3 days.

Chocolate Hazelnut Cake

Torta Gianduja

Makes 8 to 10 servings

Chocolate and hazelnut, a favorite combination in Piedmont, is known as gianduja (pronounced gyan-doo-ya). You will find many candies made or filled with gianduja, gelato flavored with gianduja, and the most famous gianduja of all, Nutella, a creamy jarred chocolate hazelnut spread that Italian kids prefer to peanut butter. Gianduja is also the name of the stock character in commedia dell'arte who represents Turin, the capital city of Piedmont.

This Piedmontese cake is dark, dense, and extremely rich.

6 ounces semisweet or bittersweet chocolate

1 2/3 cups hazelnuts, toasted and skinned (see How To Toast and Skin Nuts)

½ cup (1 stick) unsalted butter, at room temperature

1 cup sugar

5 large eggs, separated

Pinch of salt

Glaze

6 ounces semisweet or bittersweet chocolate, chopped

2 tablespoons unsalted butter

1. In the bottom half of a double boiler or in a medium saucepan, bring 2 inches of water to a simmer. Place the chocolate in the top half of the double boiler or in a bowl that will sit comfortably over the saucepan. Let the chocolate stand until softened, about 5 minutes. Stir until smooth. Let cool slightly.

2. Place the oven rack in the center of the oven. Preheat the oven to 350°F. Grease a 9 × 2-inch round cake pan.

3. In a food processor or blender, finely chop the hazelnuts. Set aside 2 tablespoons.

4. In a large bowl, with an electric mixer at medium speed, beat the butter with the sugar until light and fluffy, about 3 minutes. Add the egg yolks and beat until smooth. With a rubber spatula, stir in the chocolate and hazelnuts.

5. In a large clean bowl with clean beaters, whip the egg whites and salt on medium speed until foamy, about 1 minute. Increase the speed to high and beat until soft peaks form, about 5

minutes. With a rubber spatula, gently fold a large spoonful of the whites into the chocolate mixture to lighten it. Then gradually fold in the remainder. Scrape the batter into the prepared pan and smooth the surface. Bake 55 to 60 minutes, or until the cake is firm around the edge but slightly moist in the center.

6. Let cool in the pan for 15 minutes on a wire rack. Then unmold the cake onto a rack, invert onto another rack, and let cool completely right-side up.

7. Prepare the glaze: Bring about 2 inches of water to a simmer in the bottom half of a double boiler or a small saucepan. Place the chocolate and the butter in the top half of the double boiler or in a small heatproof bowl that fits comfortably over the saucepan. Place the bowl over the simmering water. Let stand uncovered until the chocolate is softened. Stir until smooth.

8. Place the cake on a cake rack set over a large piece of wax paper. Pour the glaze over the cake and spread it evenly over the sides and top with a long metal spatula.

9. Sprinkle the remaining 2 tablespoons of chopped nuts around the edge of the cake. Let stand in a cool place until the glaze is set.

10. Serve at room temperature. Store covered with a large inverted bowl in the refrigerator up to 3 days.

Chocolate Almond Cake

Torta Caprese

Makes 8 servings

I am not sure how this delicate cake became a specialty of Capri, but for me it is a great memento of my visits there. Serve it with whipped cream.

8 ounces semisweet or bittersweet chocolate

1 cup (2 sticks) unsalted butter, at room temperature

1 cup sugar

6 large eggs, separated, at room temperature

1½ cups almonds, very finely ground

Pinch of salt

Unsweetened cocoa powder

1. In the bottom half of a double boiler or in a medium saucepan, bring 2 inches of water to a simmer. Place the chocolate in the top half of the double boiler or in a heatproof bowl that will sit comfortably over the saucepan. Let the chocolate stand until softened, about 5 minutes. Stir until smooth. Let cool slightly.

2. Place the oven rack in the center of the oven. Preheat the oven to 350°F. Grease and flour a 9-inch round cake pan. Tap out the excess flour.

3. In a large bowl with an electric mixer at medium speed, beat the butter with 3/4 cup of the sugar until light and fluffy, about 3 minutes. Add the egg yolks one at a time, beating well after each addition. With a rubber spatula, stir in the chocolate and the almonds.

4. In a large clean bowl with clean beaters, beat the egg whites with the salt on medium speed until foamy. Increase the speed to high and beat in the remaining 1/4 cup of sugar. Continue to beat until the egg whites are glossy and hold soft peaks when the beaters are lifted, about 5 minutes.

5. Fold about 1/4 of the whites into the chocolate mixture to lighten it. Gradually fold in the remaining whites.

6. Scrape the batter into the prepared pan. Bake 45 minutes or until the cake is set around the edge but soft and moist in the center and a toothpick inserted in the center comes out covered with chocolate. Let cool in the pan on a rack 10 minutes.

7. Run a thin metal spatula around the inside of the pan. Invert the cake onto a plate. Turn it right-side up onto a cooling rack. Let cool completely, then dust with cocoa powder. Serve at room temperature. Store covered with a large inverted bowl in the refrigerator up to 3 days.

Chocolate Orange Torte

Torta di Cioccolatta all' Arancia

Makes 8 servings

Chocolate and orange make an excellent combination in this unusual cake from Liguria. Be sure to use moist, flavorful candied orange peel for this cake.

6 ounces bittersweet or semisweet chocolate

6 large eggs, at room temperature, separated

2/3 cup sugar

2 tablespoons orange liqueur

1 2/3 cup walnuts, toasted and very finely chopped (see How To Toast and Skin Nuts)

1/3 cup finely chopped candied orange peel

Confectioner's sugar

1. Place the rack in the lower third of the oven. Preheat the oven to 350°F. Grease and flour a 9-inch springform pan, tapping out the excess flour.

2. In the bottom half of a double boiler or in a medium saucepan, bring 2 inches of water to a simmer. Place the chocolate in the top half of the double boiler or in a bowl that will sit comfortably over the saucepan. Let the chocolate stand until softened, about 5 minutes. Stir until smooth.

3. In a large bowl, with an electric mixer at medium speed, beat the egg yolks and $1/3$ cup of the sugar until thick and pale yellow, about 5 minutes. Beat in the orange liqueur. Stir in the chocolate, nuts, and orange peel.

4. In a large clean mixer bowl, beat the egg whites on medium speed until foamy. Gradually beat in the remaining $1/3$ cup of sugar. Increase the speed and beat until the whites are glossy and soft peaks form, about 5 minutes. With a rubber spatula, fold $1/3$ of the beaten whites into the chocolate mixture to lighten it. Gradually fold in the remainder.

5. Scrape the batter into the prepared pan. Bake 45 minutes or until the cake is set around the edge but still slightly moist when a toothpick is inserted in the center.

6. Cool the cake completely in the pan on a wire rack. Run a thin metal spatula around the inside of the pan to release it. Remove the rim and place the cake on a serving plate. Just before serving, sprinkle the cake with confectioner's sugar. Serve at room temperature. Store covered with a large inverted bowl in the refrigerator up to 3 days.

www.ingramcontent.com/pod-product-compliance
Lightning Source LLC
Chambersburg PA
CBHW071817080526
44589CB00012B/830